concilium

THE FASCINATION OF EVIL

Edited by

Hermann Häring and
David Tracy

SCM Press · London

Orbis Books · Maryknoll

Published by SCM Press Ltd, 9–17 St Albans Place, London N1
and by Orbis Books, Maryknoll, NY 10545

ISBN: 0 334 03047 1 (UK)
ISBN: 1 57075 187 0 (USA)

Typeset at The Spartan Press Ltd, Lymington, Hants
Printed by Biddles Ltd, Guildford and King's Lynn

Concilium Published February, April, June, October, December.

Contents

Introduction

The fascination of evil is an interesting, but also a difficult, topic. We do not want to offer another issue on general questions of evil, the problem of violence and destruction, the great global problems of poverty and the cruel wars, or an issue on the problem of theodicy. *Concilium* and other theological journals have kept dealing with these topics, and will have to continue to do so in the future. We know that there are many reasons for the evil in our world. They lie in the history of our cultures and in the social relationships between our continents; they lie in the many external circumstances and at the same time in us human beings ourselves. Therefore evil keeps continuing, because the various reasons for it keep supplementing one another and increasing its potential, becoming a great web with no order, no beginning and no end. This web reproduces itself in chaotic fashion, and precisely for that reason is almost impregnable. By contrast, many generations of Christian culture imagined the evil in the world as a well-ordered kingdom. Granted, Jesus spoke only indirectly of the kingdom of Satan, but it was natural to set this anti-kingdom over against the kingdom of God. The image of a well-organized anti-ruler made its mark on cultures with a hierarchical order. Augustine developed his great historical theory on the basis of the metaphors of the 'kingdom of God' and the 'kingdom of Satan', and nowadays many Christians see the devil at work, following the most precise of plans. But presumably reality is very much worse.

Augustine already pointed out that here we do not have the external confrontation of two kingdoms. Rather, they are interwoven, and in the end, as Ignatius of Loyola emphasized at the beginning of modernity, they run through the heart of each individual. Today we must go one stage further. There is no great world plan of evil, with calculated destruction and deliberate annihilation. But there is a rampant, growing and ever-virulent web of recollections and goals, old calculations and new megalomanias, efforts reaching deep into the heart and utopian expectations. Evil has no centre, but is everywhere. It does not send out its raiding parties, but spreads like moods and rampant growths. It is present everywhere, and as a parasite of human forces, the human will and its desires, often makes its most fearful appearance where there was a hope that it had been overcome. It has often proved to be more destructive in the religions than elsewhere, and often the reasons for its power do not lie among the few who are capable of any cruelty, but among those who do not oppose it in good time.

The great disillusionment

In 1990 there was a moment when many people hoped that the abysses of our century could close up. The great ideologies had been overcome; now there had to be sufficient energy and resources to put an end to all wars and all poverty. But Francis Fukuyama's vision of the 'end of history' already seems to us to be a naive utopia. Since then literature about evil has again increased in Western countries, and S. P. Huntington's vision of a 'war of civilizations' has become the new eye-catching prognosis of world politics. We still face global clashes on the frontiers between cultures and religions. We cannot follow Huntington's theses, but we ask ourselves why so much attention is paid to new scenarios of world-political horror. Why so much new reflection on evil?

The answer to this question is not simple: one reason is that many people have been surprised by the new focal points of unrest. The former Soviet Union was not granted a peaceful way into the new era: the dirty war in Chechnia is only one of many centres of unrest which are smouldering among the many peoples on the peripheries of the former giant empire. Europe proved incapable of preventing one of the dirtiest civil wars of this century, only two and a half hours by plane from Berlin, London or Paris. The situation in Africa has not stabilized in any way and we see the horrific pictures of thousands of refugees in the primal forests every day on our television screens. The great clashes in Asia have not been brought under control, and the social war of the rich against the impoverished in the countries of Latin America is being continued unhindered. In the meantime, organized forest fires have cloaked whole countries in deadly smog, and the Global Warming Conference in Japan has just ended with virtually no success. What kind of a world do we live in?

The question for this issue

However, this question was too general for us. Not only *Concilium* but other theological journals have kept dealing with it. So we have posed ourselves a few more precise questions. It is not just the case that all of us – both perpetrators and victims – suffer under the attack of the superior forces of evil. Evil does not overcome us like a superhuman demon; we are not simply delivered over to it. It is much worse. Unless all appearances are deceptive, evil exercises a tremendous fascination on us human beings (or let us say, to be more cautious, on many individuals, communities and cultures). How does this fascination work? And are there ways of getting rid of it? This, though, is a dangerous question which can be understood cynically. Thus even during the preparation of the issue a colleague was outraged at the choice of topic. How am I, he asked, to make clear to the victims of cruelty and violence that evil has a fascinating effect? Does it not border on cynicism to reflect on this at ease when at the same time this evil is making its mark on other parts of the world? Or to put the question in another way: can those who have once heard starving children whimper, or have seen the victims of a terrorist attack bent double in their pain, or have had anything to do with the impoverished street children in Sao Paulo, still be fascinated by evil?

Therefore it needs to be noted carefully just how we put the question:

- Not from the perspective of the voyeur, who out of boredom still cynically enjoys the misery of others;
- not with the intellectual curiosity of detached analysts, who also research the horror of the world to extend the horizon of their knowledge;
- nor with the censorious view of moralists, who once again judge the world from above and confirm how much better they themselves are.

We put the question simply and solely with the *self-critical* gaze of those who know that we too constantly succumb to the spell of evil, however sublime and hidden it may be. Therefore we put the question from a perspective which is *critical of culture*, because we know that the fascination of evil has been and is produced in any of our cultures. We put it from a perspective which is *critical of society*, because we know that often some social changes or changes in the economic or political situation of the world are enough to cause a fascination with power to erupt. Finally, we put the question from a perspective which is *critical of religion*, because we know that the fascination of evil has a place in our religions, too; often it is difficult to decide whether the attention that our religions pay to evil (sin, the devil or terror at the destruction of the world) disperses and deals with the fascination for evil or makes it greater. Finally, we put the question with the *cautious hope* that ways may emerge of perhaps overcoming the pernicious fascination of evil at particular places and on particular occasions. Finally it has to become clear that as Christian theologians we will not be deterred from the great vision that God himself is the one who can deliver us from evil.

Fascination

The fascination of evil: what do we understand by 'fascination'? Current dictionaries do not give us much information here. Of course psychologists have a good deal to say about the unconscious attraction that cruelty and evil can exert on people. The experience of evil can almost intoxicate people with delusions of power. Torturers can even crave for this condition ('Being like God', 'Lord of destruction', 'Ruler over life and death'!). But our primary interest does not lie here. Current dictionaries refer us to an original religious connection. The Latin root points towards 'enchantment', 'bewitchment', 'spell'. So this is more a social and a religious phenomenon. Human beings long to be relieved of their limitations; they long to discover the mystery of the world or the cosmos; they seek a place where they can fulfil their desire, overcome their limitations, end their dependence, and finally resolve their division into body and spirit. In other words, they seek immediate experiences in which they can become themselves and at the same time be at the origin of the world. For people in industrialized societies (with the social worlds which they themselves create), that means to an increased extent that they look for ways once again to experience originality and 'reality': here it is not restriction and oppression that are the problem, but a lack of orientation and boredom.

Now there are reasons why in his famous definition Rudolf Otto, the theologian and scholar of religion, simultaneously sees two aspects in the divine: the terrifying and the fascinating (*tremendum et fascinosum*). Anxiety and hope, fear and fascination overlap; for manifestly in everything that we really fear there is also the power to overcome this fear. That explains why religions in particular are constantly concerned with the nucleus of this problem: salvation and annihilation, ways of hope and abysses, lie closely side by side. We cannot reach God's kingdom and redemption without clashing with the other kingdom. Therefore the 'fascination of evil' is a topic which is intimately related to the politics of society and culture; it is a public, religious topic.

The content of this issue

We cannot examine all the aspects in this issue. The reason for that is not just the limited space at our disposal but also the difficulty of finding appropriate authors on the international scene. That makes us all the more grateful to those who have contributed.

In the end, Part I (Analyses) has had to be limited to three articles. The first, by the theologian Hedwig Meyer-Wilmes, investigates the question of the ambivalent fascination that 'witches' exercised on the society of their time. This article makes it clear how much the phenomenon of fascination contributed to the monstrosity of the persecution of witches. Here two fascinating factors were in competition: knowledge about nature was confronted by modern rationality, the recourse to age-old knowledge by the claim of new sources of knowledge; astrology, which could not be controlled, and gentle healing by the expectations of a dominant cultural institution. Woman as 'witch' symbolizes the whole ambivalence of this process, and had not all (men) secretly succumbed to its power, they would not have taken action against this bewitchment in such an inhuman way. Thus the dark history of the persecution of witches represents the monstrous manner of dealing with those fascinations which are never discussed openly and therefore cannot be overcome until a very late stage.

The Canadian theologian Gregory Baum asks whether a non-violent society is possible. For him the question is whether it can avoid the attraction of violence. This seems impossible: even the biblical traditions with their many stories of violence confirm it. It is precisely here that the spell of this fascination lies: anyone who wants to prevent violence must manifestly use violence. So the only way to a release from fascination lies in a sober question ('Is that really the case?') and an honest answer ('That seems to be impossible'). He sees the prophetic utopia of the biblical tradition realized precisely here: this honesty alone compels us first of all to become reconciled with our histories of violence. That is difficult, but it brings liberation from the fascination of violence and opens up the only possible way, which is an ever new – and if possible ever wider – reduction of violence as a means of preventing violence. Thus the fascination is overcome by honesty and reconciliation with violence, if these are coupled with a social process which keeps reducing violence. Gregory Baum's sober but very realistic answer recalls R. Girard, who takes precisely the same course of consistent honesty and unmasking. Violence and evil must in no way nurture the illusion that they could play a final role in the overcoming of violence.

The third article in this first part (Hermann Häring) attempts to demonstrate with a view to the problem of theodicy how the fight against evil with a religious motivation – out of moralism or disillusionment – itself leads to ever new forms of wickedness and destructiveness. Faith in the overcoming of evil is put to the test time and again, and the fascination of evil keeps increasing to the point at which it becomes clear that even the most perfect theodicy of thought or action cannot solve the problem. The Christian tradition knows only one way: we must and can endure the experience of evil and our own disillusionment over God as our great question to God. This is the struggle which Job fought on his heap of ashes and Jesus fought on the cross. Did they win? Only those who in the temptation of evil do not take their eyes off God can confidently leave the answer to this question to God himself.

In Part II, these (provisional) analyses are followed by four articles which take the theological discussion further. The Latin American theologian Paulo Suess offers a survey of the disastrous history of evil in the Christian tradition on a biblical and historical basis. The great biblical utopia of a non-violent future stands over against the burden of church history. His key notions are: violence against Judaism, a mentality of crusades and missions, and a church claim to power which has constantly been fed and confirmed by the actual successes of the church and a 'Christian' culture. But Suess also shows the cloven hoof of this success. Because of its early Jewish history, from the beginning Christianity had difficulties with its own identity. Its intolerance towards alien gods and cultures and its monolithic understanding of unity made it possible for it to succumb to the magic of violence in a unique, even neurotic, way. Suess proposes counter-strategies. Their main focus is to de-demonize the other and in so doing finally discover the culture-political but also the truly religious realization of the command to love one's neighbour.

The British art historian Rosemary Wright traces one of the central symbols through which the Christian tradition has coped with evil and above all its fascination with the power of evil. There are the symbols of Satan and the Antichrist, which in past decades have undergone a renaissance not only in religious groups but also in the media of North America and Western Europe. There is a struggle of cosmic dimensions which has been reinterpreted and revised in every age. Wright demonstrates this above all from sources of the Middle Ages and Late Middle Ages (tenth to fifteenth century). For her, Satan and Antichrist are fascinating and warning symbols. But they can also become liberating symbols, provided that it is clear that we human beings still have the ability to make a choice between life-giving and destructive tendencies.

Catherine Keller reinterprets the notions of apocalyptic in a new and extremely interesting way. In fact apocalyptic is one of the most controversial trends of thought in the Christian tradition. The general view is that it usually led to anxiety, to projections of terror, to the demonization of fellow human-beings and new violence. Keller sees the problem. She gives a critical analysis of a first type, which she calls retro-apocalypse. This is a retrospective interpretation of the biblical apocaly-pse, but the approach means that this thought no longer has anything to say to us. A second type, which she calls neo-apocalypse, is more interesting. This rightly attempts to apply apocalyptic notions afresh to our time. So it sees that even now, dangers and possible disruptions of a global extent are possible. Its great problem lies in its polarizing and destructive force. The world is divided up between good and evil, and so too are human beings. Violence is legitimated. In short, that which was to be fought against is generated. The problem of fascination is not resolved, but intensified. Therefore Keller proposes a third, contemporary type which she calls counter-apocalypse. This is not orientated on a struggle against, but on a positive goal; not on the axe which is laid to the roots of the world tree, but on the great promises of Isaiah. This apocalypse is self-critical; it unmasks the naive divisions of the world into good and evil parts and thus pursues the reconciling impulse of God's Spirit, about which so much can be found in the New Testament.

The spiritual fascination of evil is thus connected with the way in which the duality of good and evil, construction and destruction, persists into the ultimate depths of the experience of God. Alexander Nava demonstrates that in a case study: the spirituality of Simone Weil. Thus talk of the hiddenness of God has both a negative and a positive significance. It means God's absence (and therefore punishment and misery and tragedy) and at the same time God's unattainable depths (and thus intimacy, expectation, enrichment). It is important to reconcile these two sides in Christian experience of God. In this way it is also possible to overcome the spell of evil; this actually lies on the quest for nearness to God.

In Part III, three conclusions follow. The German theologian and peace researcher Hans-Eckehard Bahr shows by means of a simple and impressive example from his youth work how the fascination of evil among young people in a modern industrailized city can be overcome.

The Jewish theologian David R. Blumental presents what is perhaps the most provocative article in the issue. For him the dissonance of theory and praxis is indissoluble; at the latest this has been clear since the Shoah. Therefore he calls for absolute honesty in dealing with the question of theodicy. God cannot be defended where God cannot be rationally defended. Protest is announced; not, however, protest which ends there, but protest which opens up ways of healing and reconciliation with God. With reference to the topic of this issue, that means a way which does not suppress the experiences of evil but allows them, and thus robs them of their fascination. This happens in ever-new attempts and approaches which one could call therapeutic in the broad sense of the term. It may be that in the intellectual construction of theology, for centuries we have rejected, suppressed and finally forgotten this therapeutic function of faith.

David Tracy sums up the topics of the issue and rounds it off with some basic theological reflections. He sets the fascination of evil over against the fascination of salvation and liberation. Here we as editors of the issue express our conviction that the petition 'Deliver us from evil' in the Our Father is more topical than ever. At the same time we hope that the Christian tradition – along with the traditions of many other religions – knows ways out of the spell which the struggle against evil has been under, above all in the monotheistic religions. God is the God of a peace which is not exhausted in the suppression of violence, but which flourishes out of a love of life, community and justice.

Hermann Häring
David Tracy

I · Analyses

Persecuting Witches in the Name of Reason. An Analysis of Western Rationality

Hedwig Meyer-Wilmes

Why were witches burned?

This is a question to which research, which has only turned to this genocide in recent years, has given different answers. Crises which occurred in late mediaeval societies in Europe have been mentioned: urbanization and the flight from the country, Reformation and Counter-Reformation, famines and illnesses. There has been talk of an 'epidemic of witches'; it has been said that Europe was visited by a 'mass compulsive neurosis'.[1] But this witch craze was not just a socialized psychopathy 'which made it easier for the uprooted plebeians and the city-dwellers to cope with their identity crisis by retreating into concretized forms of an interpretation of nature and with the help of misogynistic imagery'.[2] The witch craze combines rationality and irrationality, codified Christian dogmatics and the experience of everyday religion. Right at the beginning of the modern 'Enlightenment' Western rationality shows its two faces: emancipation and subjection. In other words, in the undercurrent of emancipatory reason the overcoming of domination and the creation of new situations of domination lie closely together. And the stakes where witches were burned remain a 'speciality' of Christian Central Europe. Only the witches at the beginning of modern times, who were as bound up with nature as the witches of other continents, were executed by the hundreds of thousands.

I. History and statistics

The persecutions of witches were by no means a mediaeval phenomenon. The climax of the pogroms lies between 1560 and 1630, thus already at the beginning of modern times. France, Germany, Switzerland and the Benelux countries, i.e. Central Europe, were most strongly affected. There was no institutionalized persecution of witches in Eastern Europe, southern Italy, and Ireland. In the German empire the trials of witches were concentrated around the years 1590, 1630 and 1660. The last trials of witches took place in 1782 in Switzerland, in 1793 in Poznan and in 1775 in Germany. Only in 1560, i.e. in the second half of the sixteenth century, after the first wars of religion, can one speak of a mass persecution.

Estimates of the numbers of the victims range from 100,000 to 1,000,000. Only one thing may be said to be certain, 'that apart from the persecution of the Jews, these trials resulted in the greatest mass killings of human beings by other human beings in Europe which were not the result of war'.[3] Between 1560 and 1660, 80% of women fell victim to persecutions for witchcraft. Previously the proportion of men and children was higher.[4]

Two things are already striking at this point: only the witches of the Christian West fell victim to the persecution mania of their accusers, although there were witches in other cultures. And in the witch trials almost exclusively women were tortured and killed. The perpetrators (judges, executioners, theologians, lawyers) were exclusively men. That means that any woman could burn at the stake.

At the end of the Middle Ages the relationship between nature and human beings became a problem, as a result of increasing human control over nature. Natural catastrophes and wars were the breeding ground for the hostile image of the witch. This was an image on which crises could be personalized. The anti-effects rebounded on those who as healers, specialists in herbs, midwives, mothers and widows had a great affinity to nature. Various patterns of interpretation went to make up the cultural image of witches, and three institutions are mainly responsible for them: the church, the secular authorities and the rise of (medical) science.

II. Legitimations of 'witch' as a pattern of interpretation

The beginning of modernity was governed not only by new philosophical and scientific paradigms (Erasmus of Rotterdam, Rousseau, Voltaire, Copernicus) but also by great religious revolutions: Luther and the Counter-Reformation, the rebellions of imperial knights and peasants' wars, and the Augsburg religious peace, which aimed at giving the confessions equal rights. Calvinists and Lutherans joined in the 'Union', Catholics in the 'League', and both defended their confessions with armed force. Ruined cities, depopulated villages, princely councils, ruined the peasants by additional levies and special taxes. So this was a situation in which there was need of a scapegoat to distract attention from the manifold problems.

A decisive precondition of the development of 'witches' as a pattern of interpretation was the persecution of heretics by the papal inquisition (denunciation, trial without any public accusation, torture to extract confessions, death by fire) from the thirteenth century on. It was here that magic and heresy were first linked. It was insinuated that by their pact with the devil, heretics were practising injurious magic (*maleficium*). During the fifteenth century this form of accusation was also applied to witches.

The two papal Inquisitors, Jakob Sprenger (Rhineland) and Heinrich Institoris (High Germany), persuaded Innocent VIII to promulgate a bull in 1484 in which the pope ordered under threat of excommunication that his 'beloved sons' should not be hindered in their persecutions. In 1487, Sprenger and Institoris published the Hammer of the Witches (*Malleus malleficorum*), which they prefaced to this bull, along with a forged opinion given by the University of Cologne. The first part of this opinion 'proved' the proneness of women to witchcraft with reference to biblical texts. The second part summed up the alleged misdeeds of witches: a pact with the devil, consorting with the devil, fornication with demons. The third part reads like a handbook on penal procedures:

> At a time when masses of women were being driven into the torture chambers, the church was still attempting to hold in check the new forces which had declared the old Ptolemaean system of the world obsolete and which in the wake of Copernicus were seeking to discover 'the form of the world and the symmetry of its parts'. Indirectly, however, particularly in respect of the persecution of witches, there were already signs of the later division of work: here the Catholic Church was already acting objectively in the interests of the future secular power.[5]

The secular authorities followed the spiritual authorities. Thus in 1532, Charles V created a unitary law of trials for the whole empire. Altogether, the persecution of witches lasted for three centuries; the Counter Reformation and the Thirty Years' War saw to it that the pogroms were identified.[6]

III. From healer to witch

1. *A time of transition*
Witches and healing women formed one of the most important targets of the persecution; they were thought to have 'secret' knowledge. These

'physicians of the people' were specialists in giving help at birth and in birth control, and their herbal medicine was often the usual form of medical care. Bishops and kings could resort to physicians from the university, but not ordinary people. The witches 'brewed medicine from herbs and had magical spells which protected people from all kinds of misfortunes that they expected from nature or from others, or which helped them to avenge a wrong they had suffered from another. Such a witch was attacked only if people thought that she had brought down misfortune on them.'[7]

The success of the therapy was decisive for the 'black' or 'white' magic of the healers. In the witch trials doctors functioned as experts, whereas the women healers were said to have no competence. Male scientists took over the explanation of the processes of nature, and male doctors dealt with female bodies. There was something like a shift on the part of the state and the church from natural knowledge to a science which had a rational and objective understanding of itself.

However, the transitions from the magical secret sciences to the natural sciences were fluid. An astronomer was at the same time also an astrologer; a doctor also an alchemist and an astrologer. 'If a doctor wants to give medicine to the sick, he must first note the course of the heavens and the planets at that hour. He must not fail to take account of the benevolence and the hostility of the planets towards the healing of the sick.'[8] Here a planet was assigned to every part of the body, and any diagnosis of illness presupposed knowledge of the cosmos. Moreover, illnesses which had been brought on by magic could not be cured with medicine.

> Know that of seven sicknesses which occur in these wretched times of human beings, as lassitude, problems at childbirth, rotting of limbs, cripplings, cramps, leprosy and others, at least four or five times the causes are magic and similar arts and therefore they cannot be cured by the means of the apothecary, but only with contrary magic.[9]

Thus as yet particular causes were not attributed to particular symptoms; the same symptom could have a medical or a 'magic' cause. This ambiguity of medicine then led to situations in which the power of interpretation of a disease became a life or death verdict. The ambivalence of this picture of the world can be demonstrated by a case which attracted attention in its day.

2. An example: Katharina Kepler

Katharina, mother of the astronomer Johann Kepler, the '*mathematicus* of his imperial majesty*', was accused of witchcraft for the first time in 1615.

The description of her matches the cliché of a witch and a woman: 'small, thin, with a dark brown face, a cantankerous gossip'. She was regarded as a healer. The written accusation makes her responsible for almost all the misfortunes in the village: the cattle bewitched, the father of two children killed, a young woman led out of the village to the devil, the village tailor paralysed, and so on. Johann Kepler intervened in the trial and it was stopped. However, he by no means thought his mother guiltless. Thus: 'I know a woman; she has an extremely unruly spirit, as a result of which not only did she fail to advance in her education, which is not so remarkable in the case of a woman, but she is also confusing the city authorities and causing herself wretched misery.'

He defended his mother by referring to a technical mistake in the application of Charles V's ordinance and by his astrological knowledge. In other words he possessed the keys of magic, science and politics. 'Before the court in Leonberg he exploited the unpopular calling of an astrologer and finally secured a decision that all the acts of the trial should be presented to the legal faculty of the University of Tübingen, for them to pass an opinion.'[10] Katharina Kepler was lucky. Her son's status and money made it possible for her to be acquitted in 1621. Her son, one of the figureheads of a view of the world founded on natural science, was not deterred from operating within the magical picture of the world.

> Astrologia is indeed a foolish little daughter, but dear God, where would her mother, this highly rational Astronomia, be, had she not had her foolish daughter? After all, the world is much more foolish, so foolish that this old understanding mother has to suffer the folly of the chatter and the gossip inflicted on its pious by her daughter. And the salaries of mathematicians are so low that the mother would certainly starve if the daughter did not earn anything.[11]

IV. The appropriation of the 'feminine' nature

If for a moment we leave aside the cliché of the witch as the old wizened herbal woman, there is one characteristic among the properties attributed to witches which even today permeates all the folk tales. Witches have the power to abolish the laws of nature. It is said that they not only predict the weather but also influence it; they heal illnesses and induce them, turn human beings into animals and animals into human beings, enhance or diminish sexual potency, hasten death or hold it back. 'It was certainly not possible for people in the Middle Ages to make a qualitative distinction between the healing of an illness by the laying on of hands and the administration of a herbal drink (with an effective pharmacological composition). The criterion for such differentiations was itself first the result of a social change which released human beings from the immediacy of the process of nature. The witch became its victim.'[12]

At the beginning of modern times magic was no longer a profession but a superstition. The woman always represented nature. In the eyes of the church this was an unholy alliance, and for the Enlightenment one which obstructed progress. The woman 'became the embodiment of the biological function, the image of nature, in the suppression of which the fame of this civilization consisted. To control nature without restrictions, to transform the cosmos into an infinite hunting ground, was the dream of the millennia.'[13] The modern appropriation of nature took place under the instructions of a formalized nature. And the persecutions of witches are an example of this. This was 'a campaign of persecution which was very rationally planned and which was organized in a modern way; supported by the Gestapo-like rationalized planning of the Dominicans, it was horrifyingly far-reaching and systematized'.[14]

In this constellation the witches did not have a chance. They were crushed between the church, which wanted to 'keep pale faith' as a residual bastion, and 'blossoming reason', which led to the control of nature. 'Pale faith and blossoming reason fought each other; some people got caught between them.'[15] Science emancipated itself from its origin in magic and this, too, took place at the expense of the woman. The new subject of the 'Enlightenment' was to be formed in a contrast between inner and outer natures and not in an accord with them. The magical picture of the world, which could survive through the centuries despite Christianization, 'was eliminated at the beginning of the period of manufacturing, by the triumph of modern science over theology. But its tomb was the church . . . in the truest sense, as far as the murder of women was concerned.'[16]

Those who want to see the persecutions of witches as 'bizarre and irrational'[17] fail to note that the rational found its way into convictions and minds at the cost of the former. In the persecutions of witches women became the objects of the control of nature, not only symbolically but in a real sense. Therefore the farewell to the old myth coincided with the enthronement of a new myth. 'The new person of the industrial age was the man.'[18] The loss incurred in the development of this purposive rationality at the beginning of modern times was high; criticism of it is not new (cf. Nietzsche and Bachofen). The spell was dissolved in the feminist criticism of a Western rationality which seeks to dominate inner and outer nature and shows the ambivalence of the modern project. The witches are returning. *'Tremate, tremate, le streghe son tornate!'*[19]

Translated by John Bowden

Notes

1. E. Jones, *Der Alptraum in seiner Beziehung zu gewissen Formen mittelalterlichen Aberglaubens*, Leipzig and Vienna 1912, 79.
2. C. Honegger, 'Die Hexen der Neuzeit', in ead. (ed.), *Die Hexen der Neuzeit. Studien zur Sozialgeschichte eines kulturellen Deutungsmusters*, Frankfurt am Main 1978, 21–151: 33.
3. G. Schormann, *Hexenprozesse in Deutschland*, Göttingen 1981.
4. C. Honegger, 'Hexen', in A. Lissner, R. Süssmuth and K. Walter, *Frauenlexikon*, Freiburg im Breisgau 1988, 491–500: 498.
5. S. Bovenschen, 'Die aktuelle Hexe, die historische Hexe und der Hexenmythos', in G. Becker, S. Bovenschen, H. Brackert et al., *Aus der Zeit der Verzweiflung. Zur Genese und Aktualität des Hexenbildes*, Frankfurt am Main 1977, 259–312: 290.
6. For historical information cf. E. Wisselinck, 'Hexen', in E. Gössmann et al. (ed.), *Worterbuch der Feministischen Theologie*, Gütersloh 1991, 190–4.
7. R. Radford Ruether, *Frauen für eine neue Gesellschaft*, Munich 1979, 108.
8. P. de Alto Saxo, *Wegweiser die Krankheiten zu heilen durch astronomische Konkordanz*, Frankfurt 1613, in J. Janssen, *Geschichte des deutschen Volkes seit dem Ausgang des Mittelalters*, Vol. 6, Freiburg 1903, 490.
9. Ibid., 491.
10. Quoted in M. Hammes, *Hexenwahn und Hexenprozesse*, Frankfurt am Main 1977, 19–23.
11. Ibid., 17.
12. Bovenschen, 'Die aktuelle Hexe' (n. 5), 279.
13. M. Horkheimer and F. W. Adomo, *Dialektik der Aufklärung*, Frankfurt 1969, 298.
14. Bovenschen, 'Die aktuelle Hexe' (n. 5), 291.
15. M. Michelet, *Die Hexe*, Munich 1974, 84.
16. Bovenschen, 'Die aktuelle Hexe' (n. 5), 290.
17. L. Roper, 'Witchcraft and Fantasy in Early Modern Germany', in *History Workshop. A Journal of Socialist and Feminist Historians* 32, 1991, 19–43: 21.
18. Bovenschen, 'Die aktuelle Hexe' (n. 5), 292.
19. 'Tremble, tremble, the witches have returned!', battle cry of the Italian feminists.

No Society Without Violence?

Gregory Baum

I. A difficult question

Questions dealing with violence are difficult to answer. One reason for this is that there is no agreed definition of violence. Even the authors who restrict themselves to physical violence do not agree whether this includes only the unlawful use of physical force, or whether it also embraces the lawful use of force by the police and the army. It is equally unclear whether starving populations must be understood as victims of physical violence. Are political decisions that result in famines murderous acts? Gandhi believed that hunger was the most common form of violence.

A second reason why questions dealing with violence are so difficult is that we are deeply afraid of it. As vulnerable human beings, we are afraid of the violence that may be inflicted upon us. We desire a world where we are not threatened by the use of physical force. At the same time, we are also afraid of our own capacity for inflicting violence. Not only do we, in moments of anger, envisage physical punishment to be inflicted upon the people who annoy us, but we even contemplate, in calmer moments, the physical punishment inflicted upon criminals in the name of justice. We tend to get a certain satisfaction from the powerful images of violent retribution found in the Bible, such as the plagues inflicted upon the Egyptians as reported in Exodus, and the even more imaginative punishments envisaged for the Roman empire, its clients and its elites, in the book of the Apocalypse. Because we fear the violence that threatens us and in certain circumstances enjoy the violent punishment inflicted upon people whom we regard as criminals, our reflections on violence will never be totally rational. Thinking about violence inevitably involves the emotions.

II. No consensus among social scientists

1. Aggressivity

It is, therefore, with a spirit of modesty that I ask the question whether a society can exist without violence. The first observation I wish to make is that scientists have argued about this and have not come to an agreement. Darwin's theory of evolution convinced him and many of his followers that humans have inherited the aggressivity of the animals. Since humans are destined to struggle for their survival, violence and the victory of the strong over the weak will always remain a dimension of human history. Yet Peter Kropotkin, a materialist philosopher, offered a different interpretation of the theory of evolution. He argued that humans have inherited from the higher mammals a natural bent toward co-operation. The biological fact that humans are born without claws and other organs of attack convinced him that humans are by nature peaceful co-operators. If people find their way back to the natural virtues, which for Kropotkin included altruism and self-sacrifice, they will be able to create a society without violence.

To bring out the unresolved conflict among philosophers and social scientists, I wish to contrast two opposing camps, even if many of these thinkers do not fit into either one of them. The first camp includes the thinkers who look upon human beings as selfish and aggressive, struggling to promote their own advantage. These thinkers argue that to create an orderly or civilized society it is necessary to have a government that regulates people's social behaviour and inflicts punishment on law-breakers. Human reason urges people who desire a peaceful and secure existence to favour a strong government that protects law and order. The arbitrary violence of individuals must be restrained by the rational violence of the state. In this society, rules and regulations will always be experienced by the citizens as restrictions imposed upon them, frustrating their own impulses and desires. Society remains for ever external to them, limiting their aspirations. This is the perspective endorsed by such diverse thinkers as Hobbes, Locke, the Utilitarians, Weber, Freud, and the Existentialists.

2. Co-operation

In the other camp we find thinkers who argue that people are by nature co-operators and that the formation of a peaceful society is in keeping with their profound inclination. The Catholic reading of Aristotle saw human beings orientated on the true, the good and the beautiful and hence as inwardly guided by a natural law towards the common good. Some modern thinkers argue that humans are interdependent social beings and that selfishness and greed must be attributed to the impact of unjust institutions that create inequality and undermine social solidarity. According to Rousseau, people are born with fellow-feelings and compassionate impulses, and are subsequently made self-centred by their contact with civilization. The young Marx believed that people differed from animals because their instinctual concern was for the well-being of the entire human species: he called humans 'species-beings'. Their selfishness was the product of institutions, most forcefully the free market economy. Marx believed that once the institutions fostering self-promotion were replaced by institutions reflecting solidarity, society would become free of competition and violence and the need for a law-enforcing state would disappear. Yet there are also optimistic liberal thinkers, including psychologists, who hold that people are basically good and rational and that a society without injustice and without violence is an historical possibility. Pacifists like Gandhi and anarchists like Kropotkin also belong in this camp: they believed that through self-discipline in keeping with the soul's deepest aspiration, people can become lovers of justice and peace and create a society without violence.

There are, of course, philosophers and social scientists who cannot be located in either of these two camps. Still, the point I wish to make is that philosophers and social scientists are deeply divided on the question of whether there can be a society without violence.

III. The Bible does not give a clear answer

1. *Human beings are sinners*

In regard to this question the scriptures have been read in different ways. Some traditions emphasize original sin and Cain's murder of Abel as the first transgression after the Fall. Human beings are sinners and their society will be violent. Even the redemption wrought by Christ which offers believers forgiveness and summons them to live a life of charity is unable to heal the wound produced by original sin. Christians remain sinners frustrated by the laws that protect the common good. To keep society peaceful and orderly, God empowers governing authorities to make a set of laws, supervise their application and punish the lawbreakers. In Romans 13, St Paul tells his readers that since all authority is from God, they are in faith obliged to obey their superiors. Harsh punishment of transgressors is therefore part of human history under God's providence. At one time, the church also approved of physical punishment for those who dissented from its authoritative teaching. Churches, following this interpretation of the Bible, have long defended the institution of capital punishment. For them there can be no society without violence.

2. The goodness of creation

Another reading of the Bible emphasizes the goodness of creation and interprets the fall as a wounding of human nature, not as its corruption. Relying on the prophetic promises of *shalom* in the Old Testament and the universality of Christ's salvific action proclaimed in Paul's teaching of the cosmic Christ and the Logos theology of the Fourth Gospel, these Christians believe that omnipresent divine grace offers the healing of human nature and the restoration of its original orientation on truth, love and justice. They offer an evangelical interpretation of 'the natural law', i.e. an inclination of the heart, sustained by the Holy Spirit, towards the creation of a just and peaceful society.

Christians who trust this prophetic utopia emphasize 'structural sin' or unjust institutions that exploit or oppress human beings. This concept has recently been taken up by Pope John Paul II.[1] Structural sins generate a multitude of personal sins, including violent acts. Those who derive advantages from the unjust structures harden their hearts, defend the ethically indefensible, and are often ready to use violence to protect their privileges, while the people who suffer under unjust institutions are tempted to acts of violence in their own way. If they see no way of wrestling peacefully for the creation of greater justice, they often get excessively angry, vent their frustration upon the weak and innocent or opt for unrestrained violence to overcome the system that crushes them. According to this reading of scripture, the violent acts of the privileged and of the excluded are not in keeping with their deepest inclination; these acts are rather provoked by the wounds inflicted by the structures of inequality. Christians who trust the prophetic *shalom* believe that divine grace, operative in human history, makes people yearn for a just and peaceful society.

There are, of course, many readings of the Bible that do not belong to either of these two interpretations. Yet they do illustrate the point I wish to make, namely that the Bible as such does not resolve the question whether there can be a society without violence.

IV. Fidelity to the prophetic utopia

1. Antecedent convictions

That the social sciences are unable to offer a unanimous reply to a specific scientific question is nothing unusual. This happens whenever a scientific inquiry raises issues of existential importance for the researchers which does not allow them to remain neutral. An example of this is given in a draft of the pastoral letter 'Economic Justice for All', published by the American bishops in 1986. In the draft the bishops reported that the economists they consulted were not in agreement about the causes of poverty in America nor about the manner of overcoming it. Some economists, the bishops reported, defended the idea that major reconstruction of the free market economy was an urgent necessity, while others preferred to argue that the present plight was due to faulty government policies which should and could be corrected incrementally. Because the experts were in disagreement, the bishops continued, they decided not to raise the question of how poverty in America is related to the capitalist system.[2]

In resolving social-scientific questions that raise existential issues researchers bring antecedent convictions to their work. Their fundamental attitudes, which are often not even formulated, guide their research and influence their conclusions. The question whether society can exist without violence touches upon many issues that are dear to us, our perception of human nature, our attitude towards our own society and our reaction to the punishment inflicted upon people deemed criminal. Whether we say Yes or No to this question has to do, at least to a large extent, with the social vision to which we are committed.

2. The prophetic message of scripture

The same principle applies to the interpretation of the Bible. Here too the faith conviction of the readers guides their hermeneutical approach. The contemporary debate about capital punishment is a good illustration of this principle. Some Christians defend the death penalty by referring to the violent punishment of criminals practised in biblical times, including the execution by the Holy Spirit of Ananias and Sapphira in the Acts of the Apostles (5. 1–11). Until recently the Catholic Church has supported capital punishment. Christians who oppose the death penalty turn to other biblical passages: they are particularly impressed by the ancient story that God refused to allow capital punishment to be inflicted upon Cain, the murderer of his brother Abel, and even put a mark on Cain's forehead to protect him from violence. Since the Bible embraces distinct spiritual currents, readers have to choose to which of these they want to assign priority.

I have great sympathy for the reading of scripture that privileges the prophetic and emancipatory message contained in it. As I mentioned above, this reading is based on the prophetic literature of the Old

Testament that announces God's judgment on a sinful society and God's promise of restoration, and on texts of the New Testament proclaiming that God's redemptive presence to the whole of humanity is revealed in Christ's death and resurrection. Thanks to divine mercy, creation, wounded by sin, is orientated on its full integrity. The reconciling Transcendent operative in human history summons societies in every stage of their development to reduce both the violence within them and the violence between them.

This faith, we note, does not offer a religious theory of evolution guaranteeing some sort of linear progress towards a perfectly reconciled global society. No, the gains made by one generation remain ever vulnerable to the sins of subsequent generations. Yet whatever the situation in which a society finds itself, it is divinely summoned to the reduction of violence.

3. *Other spiritual currents*

That human history is graciously destined by God to a never fully reachable earthly *shalom* is a teaching found in several texts of Vatican Council II and the World Council of Churches. The biblical foundation of this theology is sound. Yet there are also other spiritual currents in the Bible. We find in it an approval of violence, even extreme forms of it, visited upon sinners who are thought to have deserved it. There are the reports of the plagues inflicted upon the Egyptians, the stories of the genocides associated with the conquest of the Promised Land, and the apocalyptic visions of most cruel and sadistic punishment inflicted upon the rulers and elites of the Roman Empire. We have here the foundation of an ambiguous spiritual current in Christianity that allows the just to enjoy the torments of the wicked. According to St Thomas, even the blessed in heaven derive a sense of satisfaction from seeing the suffering of the inhabitants of hell.

The reading of the Bible which assigns priority to the prophetic utopia is, I think, of recent origin. It is a reading of scripture under the cultural impact of the Enlightenment ideas of human emancipation and universal solidarity. While the church at first rejected these ideas, many of its members became convinced that these ideas were in harmony with certain biblical themes and that these themes deserved to be given priority. Theologians argued that once the ideas of universality and emancipation are freed from any implication of evolution or necessity, they correspond to a Christian vision of human history. Trusting in God's redemptive presence in this history, the church eventually received the prophetic utopia in its teaching.

4. No alternative?

Fidelity to the prophetic utopia is, I think, the only theological attitude that urges societies, whatever their historical conditions, to rely less and less on violent action. Let me explain this. In general, societies permit public violence because they deem it 'necessary'. They see no alternative. During the conquest of the Promised Land, God commanded the genocide of the pagan tribes, killing not only the men but also women and children (Josh. 8.22–25; 10.28–38; 11.10, 14). Why the women and children? Because it was deemed necessary: if they survived, the tribe would rise again and seek revenge. Wars are started, persecutions are unleashed, criminals suffer physical confinement or even death, because it is deemed necessary for the safety and well-being of society. Today economic policies are imposed upon developing countries that condemn masses of people to hunger and misery because it is deemed necessary. Even the cuts in welfare support and health services in many developed countries, policies that inflict physical harm upon many, are justified in terms of necessity. We do not like it, governments say, but the international market forces make it a necessity. There is no alternative.

The prophetic utopia is a subversive principle that questions every 'necessity' legitimating violence. Replying to the question 'Can society exist without violence?' in the negative gives permission for societies to reconcile themselves with the violence they practise. Replying Yes to the question, in the name of the divine promises, challenges every society to review its practices and reduce its reliance on violence.

Notes

1. See *Sollicitudo rei socialis* (1987), par. 36.
2. The first draft of the bishops' pastoral, *Origins*, 15 November 1984, Vol. 14, no 22/23, nos. 9 and 10, p. 342.

Between Theory, Practice and Imagination

Hermann Häring

I. Fascination by confusion

Evil has many names. New names are added in every era of human history. There is no sector and no dimension of reality on which it has not left its traces: in hints, as a background reality, or explicitly. Pain, sickness and death, but also hunger, loneliness and human isolation, are evil. The damage that we do to one another, whether this is by violating physical or mental integrity, by force or manipulation, is evil. The exploitation of the defenceless, whether these are the poor or the helpless, children or women, is evil. In the end we discover the constantly recurring structures of social violence, social injustice and an organized deceit which keeps reorganizing itself, a worldwide network of mutual dependence which increasingly privileges some and drives the others into ever greater misery. It seems that no one can stop these developments.[1]

1. Fascinating names

The list of the names of evil can be continued indefinitely, since every new dimension of reality and every new branch of science discovers new conditions, traces or effects of evil; and all these have their fascination. One need think only of psychology or sociology, with their incredible arsenals of abnormality and perversion, but also their countless mechanisms and vicious circles of exploitation and distorted communication, which we take for granted, almost as laws of nature. In this list let us not forget history, which preserves the recollection of the most fearful excesses and constantly reproduces them. As can still be seen today at all the great crisis points of the world, the continuation of injustice and vengeance makes itself an unavoidable law.[2]

Finally, we must not forget the religions. As a rule they make evil a taboo and forbid it; however, at the same time they create the conditions in which violence and destruction often seem to be a divine command, and ecstasy and 'holy' passion lead to exclusion and the worse excesses. Dealing with horror and destruction – feared, threatened and produced – plays a role in all religions. In that case evil appears in the form of the way in which it is overcome: who does not come under the spell of this problem? So evil has many names.

However, we should not forget that these countless forms of injustice or destruction, of lines of death at every level of reality, existed before human beings gave this multiplicity the one name. There is no such thing as evil as such; the one word 'evil' is overtaxed by the multiplicity of the reality which it denotes; therefore 'evil' is always more than we can envisage and understand. That is an important, albeit not the decisive, reason for the fascination which it exercises.

Therefore evil also has many faces, and each seems like the mask on a hidden abyss. The fine myths of death and destruction can be deciphered as a summary of horrific damage (biographical or historical); highly dramatic narratives and plots fit for films often indicate unfathomable and pernicious structures.[3] They are only like this because in fact they are like this; because this in fact is how things are. Unfathomability and banality, a supreme sense of power and absurdity, these belong together. Even those who want to prove their unconditional freedom in evil ultimately discover no more than senseless facticity. Fascination and abhorrence manifestly belong together.

So what is evil, and what fascinates us about it? Augustine says that 'what harms' is evil: a clear and straightforward definition.[4] But appearances deceive, since no being and no clear characteristics are mentioned here. The question remains open who can be the origin and vehicle of this evil: human beings, nature, society or even God. The question remains open of what ultimately does damage: does this also include the pain which warns me of worse misfortune; or the solitude which forces me to reflect; the suffering which simply shows me my own egocentricity; or the temporary loss of happiness through which I finally grow? Is it the definitive destruction of quality of life or an insult to God? Is it humiliating living conditions which destroy people's mental or physical existence? Or do perhaps all aspects belong together, so that we cannot have them all at once? Do we not have to learn to think coherently in a sober and matter-of-fact way? But if that is the case, when should I and when may I speak of evil at all?

2. Trivialization or responsibility?

Finally, this does not answer the question whose damage and destruction is being discussed. Is it evil to accuse oppressors or to punish the guilty? How does one compare the wrath of an exploited woman with the market mechanisms under which the Third World is collapsing? So whom does evil damage? Under the same conditions, often not the strong, but the weak. Thus talk of evil often serves to hush up injustice instead of accusing those responsible. What can be hidden alongside much else under the abstract concept of 'a necessary evil' becomes trivialized. Evil becomes the foundation stone of a world which is interdependent. At the same time the trivialization of terms encourages a fascination which conjectures that behind evil there is real and unbounded life, liberation from a boring idyll of prosperity.

With power, the discovery of human freedom, which became the focal point of all reflections in European history, resists this relativization. Here an element is introduced into the definition of evil which promises clarity. Evil is deliberate destruction, deliberate cruelty. The evil one acts unequivocally, since he deliberately directs his actions towards the effect he intends and no longer leaves anything to anonymous systems or to chance. With 'modern' man, the politician and scientist, he has shaped the world in accordance with his will. This project is in process of losing its attractiveness, since the feeling of a social and structural lack of freedom has increased everywhere. That makes another problem all the more attractive: despite everything, there is a well-founded suspicion that the evil one still exists and he does not drop the mask. Often he conceals his aims. He bases them on universal rules and laws and does his work as a wolf in sheep's clothing. Or does he just inflate himself, does he just utter cruel threats, so that his problems solve themselves? Of course this type of intensification of evil develops to the point of the true villain, who damages in order to damage. For him annihilation, amorality and cruelty become an end in themselves. He appears as the monster who seeks bloodlust, the fearful ecstasy of the torturer who tortures sadistically and finds his fulfilment in so doing.[5] For the Western tradition, which thinks in terms of the individual, here at the latest the limit, and also the mystery, of evil is reached. This can be confirmed by the quantitative extent of its action, but cannot be further increased. Many people have an ambivalent attitude to it: they are attracted by it and repelled by it at the same time. Are not worlds of experience open to them which are closed to us 'normal' people?

3. Boundless abysses

Nevertheless this action has been intensified twofold during the twentieth century. First in most recent history. In our century for the first time regimes have formed in which annihilation for its own sake has become a broad social reality. The millions of victims of both world wars and the later wars in Asia and Africa, along with the abysses of deliberate, highly meaningless and irrational destruction of human beings stand for this. Auschwitz[6] and Buchenwald are its symbols, and also the Gulag archipelago.[7] The second concerns the discovery of the abysses by which European history has been shaped. There were the centuries of the practice of exclusion and annihilation, discrimination and contempt for humanity, to which people were trained, but in such a way that the codes of bourgeois respectability were not violated. Here too only symbols can be mentioned, though they are extremely real: xenophobia and the crusader mentality, misogyny and the burning of witches, megalomania and colonialism. I do not know whether this 'Christian' culture produced more inner evil than other cultures; probably not. But it has acquired a world-wide currency for itself and has powerful instruments at its disposal.

Today the systems of politics and communication, the economy and capital, have interlocked with this spirit and spanned the whole world. Thus we face developments which no one understands any longer. They cannot be excused as exceptional situations nor isolated as individual excrescences. As the Declaration of the Parliament of the World's Religions puts it, 'The world is in agony'. There are developments, abysses of human history, which confront us directly with the question what God has to do with them. Can there be any space left here for the fascination of evil?

But we must break off these reflections. Perhaps readers have followed them with a feeling of discontent because they are well-known, and because it would be too simple now to end with a reference to the mystery or, as Hannah Arendt puts it, the 'banality' of evil, or to the problem of humanity or theodicy, with Nietzsche's nihilism or Camus's cry of protest. I do not want to take this way out, but to maintain the tension. For the age of 'postmodernity', which no longer wants names or assertions, has taken a cynical pleasure in this multiplicity of answers, this confusion of concepts, this mixture of fulfilment and horror. Therefore we need to go on a bit further to proceed with some disenchantment. As a Christian theologian I am interested in three intermediate stages which play a role in this work on evil, and which could perhaps put us on the track of this strange fascination. These are the stages of reflection, action and imagination. I shall go on to show how these in particular are exposed to the fascination of the irrational, of struggle and of transcendence.

II. The fascination of the irrational

The domination of neutral and incorruptible reason is still based on the programmes of the (Western) cultures, contemporary world politics and the world economy, which continue to be directed from the West. This rationalistic constriction of perspective leads to fascination with evil, because it cannot be put within the bounds of rationality. This irrational develops its fascination with the attempt to decipher and conceptualize the names of evil. The mere fact of summarizing all destructive tendencies in the one term evil (*malum*) gives the impression of an entity which one can analyse. The definition seems to be even more precise if one locates the problem of evil as a problem of moral freedom, social or historical conditions, and thus identifies evil as moral, social or historical evil. How did that come about? The religions have always spoken about evil in myths and symbols, in rites and invocations, but the European tradition introduced a strictly ontological analysis of evil. This is largely due to the reflections of Augustine, which can be summed up under three key terms: freedom, a lack of good and the legacy of sin.[8] All three key terms can still assert themselves in present-day discussion, but they all also make the limits of all theoretical reflection clear. What cannot be assimilated here is left over as a fascinatingly irrational remnant.

1. Freedom

According to biblical tradition, it is part of the inalienable dignity of human beings, both men and women, that they are free and (if things go well) responsible for their actions. Since Augustine a new colouring found its way into this image of human beings. Augustine explained this freedom as responsibility for sinners. But the more we define freedom in terms of its dark side, as the capacity to do evil, the more terrible become the abysses which open up in this picture of humankind. Just imagine: human beings have the capacity above all to decide against their own insights. They can destroy the reality which is the basis for their lives and destroy their fellow human beings, through whom they become themselves. They can use reason for interests and goals which are hostile to life, and make reason simply a 'whore', as Luther put it. If we cannot say anything else about human beings, then that becomes the definition of them: human beings are beings who can make themselves monsters. Their dignity then becomes the sign of the deepest danger to them and the way to the worst worthlessness.

Until the beginning of modern times this abyss and all its experiences was caught up in a religious framework of reference which blunted its threatening nature. But then the dams broke. From the beginning, the modern confidence in reason was accompanied by a deep mistrust. According to Pascal we stand between the infinite and nothingness. The Enlightenment figure Pierre Bayle fled into a scepticism hostile to theory. And whereas Kant incorporates the terrible possibilities of human freedom into a system of the strictest duty, others find supreme fulfilment in it. In one work, de Sade serves as an example. He falls victim to the intoxication of an immoral, senseless but absolute abandonment by denying all humanity and any binding order.[9] This father of modern sadism sees fellow human beings only as humiliated victims. Because a final fulfilment can never be achieved, this intoxication with freedom is never satisfied. Nietzsche's avowal of the 'eternal return', of the absurdity of history (which Johann Baptist Metz called a cruel 'finale without end'[10]), finally extends the frontiers of this freedom which accepts no limitation: the fascination of an endless abyss.

2. *A lack of the good*

The second slogan in Augustine is a 'lack' or a 'deprivation of the good' (*privatio boni*). This ontological definition can persist down to the present because it avoids a positive description of evil. Instead it maintains a deep-rooted ambivalence – comparable to the notion of freedom. This definition has the effect of being a powerful battle slogan, as long as the conviction of the power of the good is victorious and indisputable. Then this formula becomes an occasion for mockery: in the end evil is weak, is nothing. As pure absence it has nothing to do with God's creation. It is of no use because it has no inner power and authority. At most it behaves like a parasite which lives at the expense of that from which it draws its nourishment, on the goodness of which it is dependent, but which it can also suck dry. So there cannot be any absolute evil, although evil constantly inflates itself and disrupts the course of this world.

This dialectic of the parasite has been played out time and again in the figure of the devil. The devil is an artist at distortion, who leads astray and corrupts, and at the same time is the representative of those who no longer notice that they must serve God and how much they may serve God. However, such a model with all its drama – played out from the desert fathers to Faust and the ascetic literature of our century – is convincing only as long as belief in God counters it strongly, indisputably, in a living dynamic. Otherwise the drama collapses in on itself.[11] The dark side of the formula gains the upper hand, the more evil is experienced as strong and overpowering. If the good fades, no more can be said of the evil either. Only now is it becoming evident how problematical this purely formal approach to evil is. Anyone who merely negates evil as a 'nothing' mistakes its effectiveness and becomes an Enlightenment-type optimist. The result is the helplessness of Voltaire, who can only react ironically to the state of the world. For him, the enlightened rationalist who does not want to give credit to this evil, all that is left is to believe in a weak God. But if God has become weak, why should we not seek our power – as the polytheists already did – in a wild, destructive Divine with perhaps a Dionysian fascination? This approach too leaves an irrational remnant which has attracted many thinkers.

3. Sinful heritage

But Augustine introduced yet a third component into his understanding of evil: with his theory of original sin he made it clear that evil is historically an extremely powerful reality – in a quite different way from that suggested by his ontological theory. Sin lives on as long as there are human beings. It is pointless here to speculate about the beginning of this evil, i.e. to go into the Adam myth and Augustine's theory of inheritance. Paul Ricoeur speaks critically of a rationalized myth.[12] Nevertheless Augustine has also been inherited at this point. In modern times, the more vigorously the Adam myth was rejected in its rationalized form, the more clearly this legacy of evil was discussed in other contexts outside the church and outside an optimistic Enlightenment. The heart of the message remained the same: we human beings live in unhappy and deadly situations and something must be done about it. But could philosophy still support theology? Hegel was the last to attempt to talk about evil in itself and to tackle the problem of evil in a comprehensive theory; after that all structures of metaphysical theory collapsed. But the fascination of evil became all the more oppressive. The analyses and explanatory models came flooding in. One need only think of Hobbes' theory of the state, which stylized the state as the 'Leviathan' which tames the human predator. One might think of Karl Marx's criticism of ideology and later that of the Frankfurt school, which made suspicion the starting point of its analyses: 'Only that which does not fit into this world is true' (Adorno).[13] The analyses of absurdity and naked despair (Sartre, Camus) were already well known at that time. The dark side of human existence was again brought to the surface, not without the effect of a tremendous fascination which existentialism with a French stamp exerted on European youth. One might recall the later analytical, sociological or psychological models of aggression, violence and the continuation of injustice (S. Freud, W. Reich, J. Dollard). Konrad Lorenz still analysed 'so-called evil' (1963); A. Polack spoke clearly of 'society and evil' (1967); E. Hacker of 'the brutalizing of the modern world' (1971). E. Fromm developed the 'anatomy of human destructiveness' (1973) and made an important breakthrough with his theory of the 'necrophilic society' by showing that industrialized societies cannot break out of this destructiveness and basically do not want to do so. P. Sloterdijk later – and then clearly and consistently – developed the 'critique of cynical reason' (1983) which in the cause of modernity has developed to the point of worshipping modern arsenals of weapons. His 'meditation on bombs' became a blasphemous, serious prayer, albeit with an apt conclusion: 'The bomb is in no way more evil than reality and is not an iota more destructive than we are. It is merely a development, a material depiction, of our being.'[14] Such books only gradually gave way to sober analyses – social, historical and psychological.

In many critical discussions the vacillation between abhorrence and enthusiasm was not decided, though there was also a wish to report about evil in a 'value-free' way. The shift towards those theories which – paradoxically enough, and reversing the circumstances in an absurd way – sought their salvation in grasping evil – seemed to be an act of despair, and failed. Nietzsche's hymn of praise to the 'new man' issued in a catastrophic welcome to National Socialism, which Nietzsche did not seek. De Sade, with a new readership in Europe and most recently called 'Kant's dark Doppelgänger',[15] wanted to invent, at least in his head, absolute evil: complete, unprecedented destruction. At the same time, as early as 1785 he observed that his goal – an absolute, bloody enjoyment grounded in complete subjection and debasement – turns into the opposite: into an absolute dependence on nature, without which he cannot enjoy anything. It need only be remarked that here we are not interested in de Sade's sexual pathology but in the fact that his books, written on the eve of the French Revolution, can also be read as the sharpest exposure and critique of a regime which was perishing. Although he cannot recognize more in it than destructive despotism, he cannot escape its fascination and makes the torment, humiliation and murder of women his supreme intellectual pleasure.

4. Absolute terror

The same is true of the hero Kurtz in Joseph Conrad's novel *Heart of Darkness* (1899), which Coppola took up in his famous film *Apocalypse Now*. This hero, too, wants to get to the basis of truth in absolute terror and to realize himself as the final authority in his tyranny over the natives in the Congo. For him, too, before his excruciating death the only communication left is the words 'Horror, horror'. From Freud's analysis of *Civilization and its Discontents* (1929) to Solzhenitsyn's *First Circle* of hell (1968), it becomes clear time and again that the veneer of morality is wafer-thin, and that the diabolical is very close to us. An abyss of evil and destruction is hidden under the thin covering of social conventions, which breaks at the slightest social earthquake. The early Ricoeur makes it clear in his own way with the means of phenomenology that we human beings cannot even succeed in just beginning to think neutrally about evil. From the beginning we are delivered over to the emotional and rational fractures of evil. Our freedom was not and is never free, but imprisoned.[16] In the worst case Hitler and Stalin become symbols of our existence; in an even more dangerous case the 'physicians' (F. Dürrenmatt), perhaps also Frankenstein or the blood-sucking vampires. The necrophilia of industrialized societies reproduces their obsessions and their fascination. It cannot be discussed away, let alone overcome, either philosophically or by theological speculation, either through moral rearmament or by biophilic therapy. The fascination of evil with the rationality of evil seems constitutive of industrial societies.[17]

Therefore what Kant was the first to say in his time is all too understandable: that all theoretical theodicies are doomed to failure. At most they can express the fascination with the question and its abysses, the infinite transcendence of evil. Therefore the theoretical question of evil becomes an endless topic of discussion, because it promises a transcending and abolition of evil in a God who does not keep this promise. What use is the solution that God himself is weak or evil, since the abysses of the world, history and reality are also grounded in him? What Luther called the 'wax nose' of such a theodicy can run in the direction of belief, but also in the direction of unbelief.[18] Nevertheless, that cannot be the last word.

III. The fascination of struggle

1. The cynicism of the detached observation

Now the biblical – and probably also the other – religions are made of different stuff. Ernst Bloch and the many more recent currents of emancipatory theologies have discovered that. For Bloch, belief in God must pale to become grey on grey if one forgets the social-critical impulse of the biblical message that he discovers in Amos.[19] Liberation theology has translated this into categories like 'preferential option for the poor and oppressed', and alongside the demonstration of solidarity has called for the praxis of struggle and the mysticism of sharing the way. Feminist theologians have formulated an uncompromising criticism of culture from this approach. This point is extremely significant for our question, since all intellectual fascination with evil from an intellectual or ethical distance is overcome by a practical encounter with it. It is enough to confront destruction and death in practice. One need only see a child dying of hunger for the cynicism of intellectual fascination immediately to become clear. To this degree the 'fascination of evil' experienced in cinemas and theatres, at the desks of academics and in the clubs of intellectuals, is already intrinsically an absurd phenomenon, which has more to do with the world in which these people live than with the horror of reality.

Can we imagine that an impoverished *campesino*, that a Thai woman who has been raped or forced into prostitution, is fascinated by the evil they experience? It seems that any intellectual fascination lives on a remnant of detached observation, on the basis of an unlived life, and therefore also on the perverse hope that at least evil still conceals a secret that will enrich our horizon. It is precisely at this point that the strength of the prophetic religions comes in. Perhaps more strongly than other religions, they – Judaism, Christianity and Islam – are concerned to change the world. They are concerned with a messianic future and thus with a practical theodicy which can also be called anthropodicy (the defence of human beings). However, they, too, are not unendangered. Anyone who propagates a practical theodicy must also know its dangers. I call them annihilation, fundamentalism, success, disillusionment and cruelty.

2. *Annihilation*

Of course these religions, too, want to understand the world; they have shown that sufficiently in their traditions. But in Christianity and Islam (and not only there) another problem now arises which occurs in many cultures. These religions are in love with success, and they stake a great deal on it. Their adherents are ready to act, to suffer and to give their all to the point of martyrdom. In the end the sacrifice of life is worthwhile for a practical theodicy; the Song of Songs (8.6) says that love is as strong as death. Can we also really attain the goal, namely the overcoming of evil? The answer is not simple.

Evil can certainly be overcome: from this great vision of humankind the struggle against evil develops its own, almost holy, fascination. But there are great dangers on the way. The first danger lies on the threshold between perception and projection, and the confusion between the two leads to the worst perversion: can I really get on the track of evil to abolish it, or for simplicity's sake am I projecting it on to people or things so as then to eradicate the people instead of evil? In the second case, human beings, societies or institutions are declared representatives of evil: they become representatives of the devil. Therefore victory over evil is sought in the annihilation of people, overcoming evil in exterminating them. The stigmatized groups of Western culture show us the fascination this perversion develops and to what fearful consequences it leads: the Mamelukes of the time of the Crusades, later the Russians or the 'gypsies', 'savages', Negroes and immigrant workers; the heretics, those of other faith and 'witches'; refugees, dissidents and 'radicals'; Jews, homosexuals and the 'degenerate'. The history of the twentieth century is full to the brim of examples of this deadly fascination. The ideologies of Fascism, Leninism and Pol Pot have lived to excess on this blinkered approach. Millions of soldiers have gone out to destroy evil with an enthusiasm on the battlefields that we no longer understand. The 'holy war' is not a Muslim invention (and is not identical with destruction there), but a phenomenon widespread in all great cultures.

3. Fundamentalism

Islam rightly requires the battle against evil (*jihad*) to begin in human beings themselves. Only in this way can unconditional dedication to the holy cause grow. But that can also give rise to a dangerous, what I would call a fundamentalist, temptation. We indeed make the overcoming of evil our cause; we commit ourselves to the cause and identify with it. But by assimilating our interests to the overcoming of evil, and thus dedicating ourselves wholly to that goal, a reverse dynamic is also set in motion. The goal is assimilated to our identity, our expectations and notions. Characters, goals of groups, religious traditions or cultural codes determine the way. We define what has to be evil. The Jewish social philosopher Z. Baumann points out that any compulsion to order results in even greater chaos.[20] Ecstasy follows disciplining; those who want too much orthodoxy will reap heresy. Even more dangerously, we compel resistance and aggression by our ideas of order. Thus we create the pernicious thing that we then fight. Fundamentalism is not just a reaction to the uncertainty of modern men and women, but also the legacy of a rationalizing way of thinking in terms of order, often an inquisition from below.

That sketches out the problem: the razor's edge between extreme matter-of-factness and extreme dedication can be trodden safely only by those who with the utmost degree of modesty and self-criticism give others their freedom and act with an explicit and constant readiness for self-correction. As soon as we assimilate the goal to our programmes and then stabilize these programmes so that they reinforce our battle strength, we succumb to a fascination which brings about more destruction than help.

4. Success

Now fundamentalism has many causes. But at all events it means that the balances between commitment and a readiness for correction, between conviction and modesty, disappear. The overcoming of evil is then identified with particular personal view, with the fixed statements of a religion or with the norms of a culture. This danger is all the more seductive, the more successful the battle. In that case the fundamentalism of personal conviction then develops into what E. Drewermann has called the 'institutionalism' of highly organized religions. Thus we know the paradoxical phenomenon that in their zeal to save, Christianity and Islam became prototypes of world conquest; that the religion of love of neighbour developed an aggressive power politics, waged wars and propagated an unbending dogmatism and an inhuman moralism. Certainly that is really not the whole truth about Christian faith. But in an unqualified commitment to the good, the dangerous fascination now arises of the good and successful programme, the only true vision, the legitimation of wars for the 'good cause'. This danger has moved on into modern theories of society. 'Real socialism' took it over. A plannable future has a fascinating compulsion. That is why Hans Jonas – in deliberate contrast to Ernst Bloch's *The Principle of Hope* – wrote an ethics with the title *The Principle of Responsibility*. Promise, according to Jonas, all too easily turns into threat. He wants to avoid messianic, political and social projects for the future – in a supposed battle against evil – leading to the euphoria of a destructive actionism.

However, at this point it is important for us to look closer. So far we have been speaking of an honest enthusiasm for the supposed good. That may indeed often have been the case; the fascination of evil for the sake of good is usually more underhanded and more sublime. Representatives of order are usually not naive but mistrustful, and with good reason. This too can be explained in the light of the aim of a practical theodicy. I remarked that a theoretical theodicy is impossible, and this impossibility makes people prone to the intellectual fascination of evil. We must now ask whether a practical theodicy is possible. Many would say that it is. Cannot Christians refer to God's promise? Is not the glory of God the salvation of humankind (Irenaeus of Lyons), and in his promise to human kind has not God staked everything on our mutual solidarity? Reality speaks a more differentiated language. Certainly no liberation theology will give up the obligation which it takes for granted, its preferential option for the poor and those with no rights, but it is one of its precious experiences that commitment to one's fellow human beings brings fulfilment even when it does not lead to success. Here a tension comes to light which is often not discussed sufficiently, but which we Christians must know from the history of Jesus of Nazareth: a commitment to a more human future does not necessarily lead to the success for which we strive; complete success is almost impossible.

5. Disillusionment

A lack of success in commitment to the good: from a psychological perspective that is an extremely dangerous thing. It is the failure to cope with lack of success in a most sacred commitment that nurtures the germ of disillusionment, of annoyance, of bitterness in us. The beginnings of this problem can already be studied in the letters of Paul, for example in Paul's battle against observance of the Torah (Gal. 5). Here emotions and reactions of harshness arise. Then the lack of success is readily explained in terms of the 'works of the flesh' (Gal. 5.19–21), of a lack of understanding (Rom 2.20), perhaps also of lukewarmness (Rev. 23.16). 'You have the devil for your father' (John 8.44), is not the most friendly of Jesus' sayings. Disillusionment is directed outwards. Those addressed are confronted with the disillusionment of the one who addresses them; all the problems are projected on to them, so that with their (supposed) guilt they allay the disturbing phenomenon. That is a more frequent and more concrete way, which R. Girard has described in a highly developed theory. Where goals are aimed at (and missed), potential violence comes into play; religions are no exception here. Because of their goals, they in particular know a religious fascination with power and violence. Frustrated men and women can develop an almost raging zeal for justice, an increasing recourse to compulsion if care and admonition are to no avail. A lack of success leads to a fascination with a harsher, because apparently more effective, way. Evil is then fraught with evil. The more the churches have understood themselves in terms of their institutions, the more they have succumbed to this fascination. Here too the law of the unlived life comes into play.

6. Cruelty

Here, too, there are movements and transitions. Dostoievsky's Grand Inquisitor is prepared to send away Jesus, the best of human beings. Dostoievsky has made the Grand Inquisitor the symbol of a heartless dogmatism which no longer wants to have anything to do with Jesus. Robespierre becomes the symbol of the one who literally walks over dead bodies for the sake of a political order, i.e. an abstract good, after the guillotine had been promoted as the machine of humane dying. In the Paris of those years dying, which was meant to secure a new freedom, became a mass commodity; fascination with this event, too, has not diminished. On the contrary, like the burning of any witch, any guillotining could be certain of an enthusiastic public.

This is the point at which evil gradually loses all shyness and self-distortion. At the latest in the twentieth century, among the self-styled engineers of our society, the mystery of evil, the intoxication with blood, the fascination of sadism, can become a reality undistorted by politics: destruction for its own sake begins. The life which is unlived, the injustice experienced, the heaped-up disillusionment satisfy themselves. The necrophilic structures of industrialized societies throw off their masks. Hitler finally takes the fantasies of evil seriously. We know that torturers can be intoxicated by their torturing; the humiliation of others becomes an addiction.[21] Many soldiers in past wars also took a satanic pleasure in killing, as we know: Germans in Russia in the Second World War, the Japanese in Korea, the Americans in Vietnam, others in civil wars in their own countries. The true sadist is not de Sade with his crimes imagined in prison. The true sadists are those obsessed with order in chaotic times, the everyday torturers, the onlookers at public liquidations and shootings, those who perpetrate massacres.

Time and again there are people who torture as in ecstasy and bloodlust, who kill as in a delirium or enjoy at their desks their power over life and death. Evidently there is the crossing of a last boundary beyond which people are their own measures. The effect of violence, murder and wild destruction, the realization of the unprecedented, seem to create a feeling of one's own power and superiority which only knows itself. Naked evil takes the place of fighting for the good and is experienced as removing the limits of one's own possibilities. Evil then promises and gives not only the fascination of unconditional superiority but also a compulsion to confirm this superiority time and again. Shortly before his suicide, Hitler declared that the German people had not proved worthy of him. It is not surprising that when in an absurd reversal of circumstances Bataille spoke of 'holy evil', he was at his desk imagining it as the transgression of all morality. In 1946 he was taught better. Now he knew that no aimless transgression of abstract morality but Buchenwald had become the indelible sign of evil as a satanic entity. Is there also a fascination with evil here? There is at any rate until the moment when evil has destroyed itself, and at all events as long as one does not think of the victims which it pulls down with it into the abyss. But the fascination of this realized evil remains possible, because practical theodicy, too, never leads completely to its goal, and because success and failure are often interwoven to the point where they can no longer be distinguished.

IV. The fascination of transcendence

1. *Final rejection*

But a remnant remains. As I said, evil is an open concept and therefore one which cannot be defined. It contains not only the experiences of manifest and final destruction, inhumanity and public injustice, but also elements of subjective judgment, of projection and therefore of deception. We always understand evil, whatever it may be, as always being the same, that which may not be in any circumstances: a moral verdict is associated with it. Whereas Taoism, for example, wants to balance out good and evil, like all opposites, and whereas for Jung it was part of the health of human beings that they should accept their shadow sides, in our culture evil remains attached to a definitive element. Evil is not only that which damages and therefore must be held in check, but also that which ultimately drops out of the order of the world and therefore may not exist in any circumstances. The developments of the twentieth century have proved this postulate right.

As a Christian I agree with this basic structure because without reservations I want a just society and world with a future, because I am convinced by the messianic promise of the biblical faith. At the same time I know – and this will be demonstrated – how difficult it is to live with this resolute will and hope, with commitment to such a just future. The danger that this will for the good will turn, as we saw, into the fascinating compulsion of a destructive world, is ever present. Whether we are Christians or not, all of us who live in hope of a better future evidently live by the boundless and ever-endangered vision of a reconciled world, in other words from a superfluity of a desire for fulfilment which is never met. Anyone who knows 'only' practical theodicy as a goal will not survive the battle for the good without bitterness and hardness, and will not know whether he (or she) is not somehow seeking evil as a means of overcoming it, in other words whether he or she is not succumbing to the fascination of such a possibility.

2. *Religion*

Religion arises in the split between a world obsessed with violence and driven by death on the one hand and the expectation of this reconciled future on the other. If it does not succumb to the onslaught of evil, it celebrates the experience that despite all defects, reconciliation and love already exist here and now. It tells us that it is worth while fighting for a better world, even if the reward is still to come. If we believe psychologists, six-sevenths of our world of notions and hopes consists of unconscious dreams; they are activated. So is religion an opiate? If my view is correct, comfort is only the basis for real religious work. Religions above all work on the fact that our expectations always remain unfulfilled, that our theodicy does not succeed even in practice. They preserve us from the fascination exercised by an unfulfilled life. For Hans Küng, the borderline between faith and superstition lies precisely at this point. True religion 'does not recognize anything as absolute authority that is relative, conditioned or human, but only the absolute itself, which in our tradition we have called God since time immemorial'.[22] Where this boundary is crossed, superstition and its dangerous consequences begin.

Here the healing counter-experiences of a successful faith start. In this trust the frontiers of our action are worked through, the bitterness which arises is dissolved, and unconditional faith in a successful future is strengthened. The perspectives of those without rights is protected as a creative source. Is that a way of robbing the fascination of evil of what nourishes it? According to R. Safranski, the totalitarian ideologies of this century and the more modern fundamentalisms 'claim to know what holds the world together; they want to grasp the whole and reach after the whole person; they give the security of a fortress with observation slits and embrasures'. By contrast, again according to Safranski, religion 'directs the horizontal quest of human beings into the vertical. If there is a God, human beings are freed from being here for one another. They can shift their lack of being on to one another and make themselves mutually responsible for it, if they feel strangers in the world.'[23] I believe that once the theodicy question has theoretically failed and has been greatly endangered as a practical undertaking, we can sustain it only by looking towards God.

3. An end of fascination

So now do we have a cheap consolation which helps us get over all problems? No, no fit religion can give the impression that God solves our problems and does not take the burden of our freedom seriously. Therefore a problem remains open here. Here we need to refer back to Kant. He asserted that theoretical theodicy was at an end. He conceded that Job, whose protest before God he calls an 'authentic theodicy', was right: human beings must be able to cry out their pain. God must hear the cries of a Job and the complaints of mothers whose children have died prematurely. Therefore even at this last stage, the problem of evil has not been simply solved.[24] We cannot forbid anyone to recognize the abysses of the world in God. The first Christians associated the advent of the Messiah with apocalyptic pictures of terror which we would very much like to suppress today.[25] A whole Christianity could not imagine God without Satan as his fearful opponent. Our hopes continue to be stamped by this tension.

Therefore the only thing we can do is to confront God with the burden of our present and make him respond. Evil will not be resolved even in the kingdom of our dreams. Satan, the anti-God of destruction, the lord of contempt for others for the sake of a better humanity, will also perform his play there, as we know from the Apocalypse. But we can play the game of fascination to an end there and get out of it by – in remembrance of the death of Jesus – also concentrating all evil in the God who is our hope.

What should that mean? In this connection Johann Baptist Metz speaks of the 'God mysticism' of Jesus, who trusted wholly in God and was abandoned by him. The very problem of theodicy described here, the fascination of evil, is the other side of this godforsakenness. Jesus' God mysticism is, as Metz says, 'in a unique way a mysticism of suffering over God. His cry on the cross is the cry of the one who has been forsaken by God but who for his part had never forsaken God.' According to Metz, 'That points inexorably to Jesus' God mysticism. Jesus sustains the divinity of God.' In the godforsakenness of the cross he affirms a God who is more and other than the echo of our wishes, however ardent; who is more and other than the answer to our questions, however hard and passionate, as in the case of Job, and finally as in the case of Jesus himself.[26]

It is at this point that the decisive turning point comes for Metz. Does this faith bring happiness? Metz doubts it. The problem of this world is not simply solved; evil does not simply disappear from sight. But in his view this faith which is maintained by Jesus indicates a way. 'The experience of God inspired by the Bible is not a mysticism of open eyes, nor is it a perception which relates to itself, but a heightened perception of the suffering of others.' That is the way which Christian faith has to offer. Anyone who sees the suffering of others and helps it is rid once and for all of the fascination of evil.

Translation by John Bowden

Notes

1. H. Haag, *Vor dem Bösen ratlos?*, Munich 1978/1989.

2. H. Häring, *Das Problem des Bösen in der Theologie*, Darmstadt 1985; A. Görres and K. Rahner, *Das Böse. Wege zu seiner Bewaltigung in Psychotherapie und Christentum*, Freiburg 1982.

3. P. Ricoeur, *Finitude et Culpabilité* I: 'homme faillible'; II. *La Symbolique du Mal*, Paris 1960.

4. '*Id quod nocet*' (*De mor. Man.* II,3,5; PL 32, 1346).

5. W. Sofsky, *Traktat über die Gewalt*, Frankfurt 1996; H. Arendt, *Eichmann in Jerusalem, Ein Bericht von der Banalitat der Bösen*, Munich 1986.

6. H. Mulisch, *De ontdekking van de hemel*, Amsterdam 1992.

7. A. Solzhenitsyn, *The Gulag Archipelago*, London and New York 1974.

8. H. Häring, *Die Macht des Bösen. Das Erbe Augustins*, Zurich 1979.

9. Marquis de Sade, *Juliette*, London 1991.

10. J. B. Metz, 'Time without a Finale', *Concilium* 1993/5, 124–31.

11. H. Haag et al., *Teufelsglaube*, Tübingen 1974.

12. P. Ricoeur, 'Die Erbsünde. Eine Bedeutungsstudie', in *Hermeneutik und Psychoanalyse. Der Konflikt der Interpretationen* II, Munich 1974, 140–61.

13. T. W. Adorno, *Negative Dialectics*, London 1973; M. Knapp, '*Wahr ist nur, was nicht in diese Welt passt.*' *Die Erbsündenlehre als Ansatzpunkt eines Dialoges mit Theodor W. Adorno*, Würzburg 1983.

14. P. Sloterdijk, *Kritik der zynischen Vernunft* I, Frankfurt 1983, 252–61: 259.

15. R. Safranski, *Das Böse oder: Das Drama der Freiheit*, Vienna 1997.

16. Ricoeur, *Phenomenologie* I, ch. 4.

17. E. Fromm, *The Anatomy of Human Destructiveness*, New York 1973.

18. R. Faber, *Der Selbsteinsatz Gottes. Grundlegung einer Theologie des Leidens und der Veranderlichkeit Gottes*, Würzburg 1995; B. Gesang, *Angeklagt: Gott. Über den Versuch, vom Leiden in der Welt auf die Wahrheit des Atheismus zu schliessen*, Tübingen 1997; G. Streminger, *Gottes Güte und die Übel der Welt*, Tübingen 1992.

19. E. Bloch, *Atheismus im Christentum*. Frankfurt 1973, Preface.

20. Z. Baumann, *Dialektik und Ordnung. Die Moderne und der Holocaust*, Frankfurt 1992.

21. Sofsky, *Traktat über die Gewalt* (n. 5), especially chapters 5 (on torture) and 10 (on massacre).

22. H. Küng and J. Ching, *Christianity and Chinese Religion*, New York and London 1989, 56.

23. Safranski (n. 15), 326f.

24. W. Gross and K.-J-Kuschel, '*Ich schaffe Finsternis und Unheil!*' Ist Gott verantworlich für das Übel?, Mainz 1992; G. Theobald, *Hiobs Botschaft. Die Ablösung der metaphysischen durch die poetische Theodizee*, Gütersloh 1993.

25. O. Marquard, '*Was dürfen wir hoffen, wenn wir hoffen dürften?*' *Eine Eschatologie* (3 parts), Gütersloh 1993–96; E. Schüssler Fiorenza, *Revelation. Vision of a Just World*, Edinburgh 1993.

26. J. B Metz, 'Theodizee empfindliche Gottesrede', in id. (ed.), '*Landschaft aus Schreien.*' *Zur Dramatik der Theodizeefrage*, Mainz 1995, 81–102: 99f.

II · Theological Approaches

Overcoming Evil. The Ambivalence of Biblical Notions of Salvation in History and the Present

Paulo Suess

Modern utopias of deliverance from evil have not been fulfilled. World wars and campaigns of ethnic extermination, Holocaust and torture, exploitation and extreme poverty, drug terrorism and destruction of the environment characterize the dark side, the fallen history, of this century which is coming to an end. Here alongside public evil there is a tendency to privatize evil in the home of 'Adam's family'. This evil which has become domestic does not require any great story, any particular motivations; it requires neither pathos nor legitimation. Whereas the Thirty Years' War was still about true religion, and the bloody revolutions up to and including terrorism were, or at least claimed to be, about freedom and liberation, evil has now also become private enjoyment and a way of overcoming boredom. It is no longer any great matter, but unmotivated spontaneous arson on those who happen to be around.[1]

We live in a divided situation in which both the fascination of knowledge and the fascination of ignorance can contribute to evil. The stages of violence match the stages of development of particular cultures almost symmetrically. Vulgar pleasure in public executions, or a delight in them stemming from an obsession with justice, is associated with pleasure in almost unmotivated cruelty. In such an evil situation the ambivalence of all the promises of deliverance which have been tried out in history, including those in the Bible, becomes particularly clear. Nevertheless, it is precisely because of them that human beings are not content with the destruction of life. Those who keep an eye on the eschatological horizon of deliverance from evil can evidently find the liberating forces which are needed by people who seek deliverance from it to rob historical evil of its legitimation.

I. Impulses from scripture

Deliverance from evil and its consequences is a central promise of
scripture. The evil which appears in life and creation is fundamentally
opposed to its divine author. The summons to collaborate in history to
overcome evil is a call to be responsible for a world which is endangered by
evil and an invitation to praise its creator, so that God can be all in all.

1. The project of creation

In the biblical view, evil is a destructive act on the project of creation
which is related to its subject. It can transform itself into the diffuse
anonymity of structures, where it becomes virulent as 'powers of death',
'structures of sin' (Santo Domingo 13 and 243) and 'institutionalized
violence' (Medellin II, 15). The process of healing the evil in history is a
process of opening (Isa. 6.10; Mark 7.34ff.); it is a salvation history which
takes on its character from the partnership between God and human
beings. Israel has experienced the liberating action of its God in election
from anonymous insignificance and in liberation from slavery, in the
covenant and settlement in the Promised Land, in the exile and finally in
the homecoming from captivity. But Israel also understood this act of
liberation cosmically as a creative intervention by God to remove aimless
chaos. The covenant God of Israel promises not only a new land, but also a
new heart in a new covenant (Jer. 31.31; Ezek. 36.26).

Chaos has an outer dimension and an inner dimension. Outward
dispersion and inner disruption are its indicators. Therefore deliverance
from evil is treated in the Bible as an ordering and life-saving action
between God and human beings; as a battle against outward slavery,
inward confusion and structural disorder; as God's support through grace;
and as a resolute commitment by human beings on the side of those who
suffer the burdens of subjectively incurred and structural sin in a special
way, through indifference, exclusion and exploitation.

2. Human action

According to scripture, evil is not a fate, but must be responded to by
human beings themselves. The devil is indeed a 'murderer from the very
beginning' and 'father of lies' (John 8.44), but he does not reduce human
responsibility to fate or the compulsion of structures. Death came through
a human being (cf. I Cor. 15.21). Death has many faces. Therefore evil is
not just about physical destruction, fratricide and genocide, but about
malicious envy, vengeance and greed, about refusing to give oneself, and
shutting oneself up in law, tradition, rite and sacrifice. Finally it is about

the destruction of images of the world and ways of life, about ethnocide, contempt and indifference, the exploitation and exclusion of others.

On the broad scale between voluntary self-sacrifice in martyrdom and masochistic self-destruction, and between the sacrifice of others in the service of and under the supposed compulsion of the deity and the destruction of other life as an expression of power, the destruction of life can be experienced as pleasurable, i.e. as subjectively fascinating. Human beings are 'prone to evil' (*Gaudium et spes* 13). They can live out their fascination with this structural tendency or they can endure it painfully, trusting that God will forgive sins and deliver them from evil.

3. The claim and task of Christianity

The petition in the Our Father (cf. Matt. 6.7–15b) articulates a 'remission of sins' and 'deliverance from evil' in the two ideally conceived situations of the year of jubilee and the kingdom of God. In the synagogue in Nazareth Jesus refers to the unrealized ideal of the year of jubilee and declares it programmatically to be his life's project (Luke 4.16ff.), as a year of grace for the poor, the deliverance of captives and healing of the blind. In Jesus' preaching about the kingdom of God, the project of the jubilee year takes on a universal, historical-eschatological dimension. The advent of the kingdom of God represents the break with evil in its structural form, and in its guilt which is a personal responsibility. Jesus of Nazareth proclaims it as the persistent vision of the possibility of successful life.

Now Christianity makes the claim to be fulfilling the two 'ideals' –jubilee year and kingdom of God – by announcing the deliverance from evil which has finally taken place in Jesus Christ. This makes other redeemers and ways of redemption very nearly idols and idolatry. They can exercise a fascination which deafens and blinds, but cannot bring illuminating insight. They have deaf ears; they have eyes with which they do not see (cf. Isa. 6.9; Jer. 5.21; Mark 8.18). In the Synoptic Gospels the healing of the blind is the last and especially significant healing miracle (Matt. 20.29f). The blind person who is healed is a seer, a follower and a fighter at the same time. One must do good and fight evil. Christianity constantly keeps struggling with opposed tasks. It must be in this world but not of it; it preaches fear of God and love of God, mercy and justice, the divine final cause and human responsibility, peace and the sword, prayer and work, the option for the poor and universal salvation for all.

II. The burden of history

Historically, we can identify at least three different groups to which the biblical message of deliverance was addressed: Judaism, the pagan non-Christian environment, and finally the members of the Christian religious community. Demarcation from the fathers in faith (Judaism), superiority to others/strangers and a patriarchal authoritarian way of preventing others from really growing up are indicators of a weakness in identity and faith which keep appearing in the course of history.

1. Violence against Judaism

Endured violence was mimetically incorporated in Christianity at a very early stage and then handed down, at first verbally and then in actions in history. After the stoning of Stephen, the Jews were publicly attacked as murderers of God (Acts 7.52). We find the continuation of this anti-Jewish discourse which was authorized by the church in the church fathers, for example in Augustine.[2] In 388 Bishop Ambrose defended those who had set fire to the synagogue of Kallinikon (Euphrates) against their condemnation by Theodosius. The Bishop of Milan described the synagogue as 'a place of unbelief, the home of godlessness, the lair of madness condemned by God himself'.[3] He himself, Ambrose, would have synagogues destroyed in Milan, had this not already happened long before. Now it is no longer the synagogue which wants to show God a service by murdering Christians, but Christians who believe that they can show God a service through wars of faith (cf. John 16.2).

Killing and being killed for the purpose of redemption is justified as service of God by Bernard of Clairvaux and in the apologetic literature for the Crusades. The soldiers of Christ fight 'without the slightest fear of sinning because they exposed themselves to the danger of death or killed the enemy. For them dying or killing for Christ is not a crime, but brings with it great honour.'[4]

2. The crusade and mission mentality

After Augustine's *Retractationes*, theologians and missionaries legitimate the use of force with the phrase 'compel them to come in' (Luke 14.23).[5] Underlying this is justification through a 'positive responsibility' for the salvation of others. Thomas Aquinas thinks that physical chastisement which leads to the conversion of heretics is a good deed.[6] With similar arguments José Acosta, the first Provincial of the Jesuits in the vice-kingdom of Peru, as early as 1576 calls for a 'new evangelization' which has to be accompanied by soldiers. In particular the 'more primitive' natives had to be forced into the kingdom of heaven, in the way one uses with children who oppose doctors and teachers.[7] José de Anchieta (1534–1597), one of the first Jesuit missionaries in Brazil, also reported to Diego Laynes, the general of his order: 'For this kind of people there is no better preaching than the sword and the iron rod . . . for the "compel them to come in" must needs be fulfilled.'[8]

3. The church's claim to power

Yves Congar has shown how in the course of church history reference was made time and again to a verse from the call narrative of the prophet Jeremiah to justify universal spritual and secular power: 'See, I have set you this day over nations and over kingdoms, to pluck up and to break down, to destroy and to overthrow, to build and to plant' (Jer. 1.10).[9] This verse, which later became a formula for the sending out of papal legates, was then often quoted in connection with the papal authority to bind and loose (cf. Matt. 16.19), in order to safeguard the papal *plenitudo potestatis* (Bernard of Clairvaux) over *gentes et regna*. As late as 1942, at the time of the Second World War and the Holocaust, the Roman Congregation of Rites published a special mass for papal saints in which Jer. 1.10 was quoted.[10]

III. Difficulties with identity

From the beginning, Christianity understood itself to be incompatible with other religious traditions. The 'putting away of strange gods' (Josh. 24.23) was an indispensable condition of salvation, for which Israel and the church struggled equally. 'Strange gods' threatened the identity of Christianity from outside, in the form of pagan religions, and within, in the form of popular religion.

1. Strange gods?

But what are 'strange gods'? The divine mediators of traditional religions must not be confused with gods, nor must those who venerate them be misunderstood as polytheists. The sweeping claim by the African Cardinal Gantin that the traditional religions of Africa have always been 'radically monotheistic' can only be understood as a concession that for centuries the African religions have been wrongly evaluated.[11]

One day an Indian cardinal, with the authority of his office to make classifications within the church, will advance this claim for Indian religions. Truths have a temporal nucleus. Their competence to define is limited by historical points of decline, social spheres of validity and cultural patterns of expression. This also applies to the claim that Brazilian popular Catholicism is polytheism, and that Christianity is now itself reproducing the polytheism that it encountered and fought against in the religion of ordinary people.[12]

2. False images?

In parallel to the Reformation dispute over images, in conquered America there was a fight against false images. Bernal Diaz, who reported the *Conquista* of Mexico, describes how after the destruction of the Totonakes' statues of their gods and amidst the tears of their priests, Cortes set up in their sanctuary an image of Mary and an altar, and had a mass celebrated there.[13] The gods of the pagans were regarded as demons. Their sacrifices were regarded as sacrifices to demons (cf. I Cor. 10.20). But whoever destroyed the divine images of the others also destroyed the others physically. The frontiers of 'Christian' Europe and 'Catholic' Latin America are marked in blood.[14]

3. Which unity?

In Western thought, the normativeness of culture has continually undermined the normativeness of faith. 'The one is the whole', runs the Neoplatonic axiom which found its way into Christianity. The 'one', not thought of as an articulated sum of multiplicity – turns into a hierarchy the brotherly and sisterly equality of human beings, their polar sexuality and cultural difference. But a public recognition of the difference between sexes, brothers and sisters, generations and cultures, is an essential presupposition for the containment of violence. As a complement to the Neoplatonic concept of unity, a concept of identity which excludes the third party, going back to Aristotle, burdens Christianity.

The binding alternatives, either Christian or pagan, true religion or idolatry, are pointers to violence because they exclude complementarity. But because the whole mystery of God cannot be expressed in any religion and culture, the Jewish-Christian tradition, too, cannot be enriched by the experiences of God which are had in other religious and cultural contexts. One cannot make a claim to be proclaiming a message of redemption to a people and at the same time require it to forget its traditions or to locate these very traditions before or outside the history of salvation. Salvation history as universal history under post-colonial conditions must always be thought of at the same time as the sum of many salvation histories.

IV. The logic of sacrifice as the service of God

1. The magic of violence

In Christianity we keep encountering a vulgar theology of the cross which does not get by without those bloody human sacrifices which it denounced and attacked, for example among the Indios of Mexico and Brazil. A 'bit of' violence against 'un-Christian others' is said not to be the lesser evil, but an eschatological good deed. Violence for the purpose of redemption is the service of God. The liturgical character of physical violence as a sacrifice is saving service for human beings.

'In their history,' says Albert Görres, 'the churches have practised much calumniation of God, for example when with the authority that has been given them they have declared that it is the will of God for crusades to be waged, witches to be tortured, real and supposed heretics to be burned, scholars to be deprived of their freedom.'[15] The justification that the violation of the rights of others is service of God is archaic and pre-Christian, and falls far short of the basic ethical reciprocity which is practised in any tribal people. Violence against others and destruction of the traditions of others is not a contribution to deliverance from evil, but itself forms a magical act which serves idols. Magic has no memory, knows no history and does not deliver from evil. The logic of sacrifice as serving God denies the central axis of Christianity, gratuitousness. Solidarity and self-surrender do not have an eye to the possibility of incorporating others into one's own religious community or one's own heaven.

2. Solidarity instead of the logic of sacrifice

So a distinction has to be made between enforced sacrifices and self-sacrifice. Witnesses in blood (martyrs) are not victims to be rescued against their will or representative lambs of God. To this degree the mimetic 'everything has its price' logic is not just about calumniation of God but about the denial of God, about the displacement from grace of the Author of life.[16] Where God is forced out, the vicious circle of ritualized violence begins. Moreover that has also been demonstrated in the legitimation of slavery as a 'Christian good deed', which is grounded in the Bible, and 'a great miracle of divine providence and mercy'.[17] Slavery by Christians opens up the door to redemption. A slave who is a redeemed Christian is better than a free pagan who is damned in the literal sense. The dossier of slavery and human sacrifice has a contemporary relevance.

On the occasion of the deportation of Jews to the concentration camps in October 1941, Cardinal Faulhaber of Munich wrote to Cardinal Bertram of Breslau: 'Scenes are taking place here . . . which in the chronicles of this time will one day be paralleled with the transports of African slave-traders.' To this Bertram replied that there was need 'initially to concentrate on other wider interests which are of more importance to the church',[18] for example those of the 'Catholic youth'. In the face of the industrial destruction of the other, however, in 'catholic' terms it would have to be said that no one is excluded from universal solidarity nor may anyone be sacrificed silently – even at the price of failing to give help.

V. Neurotic fascination

1. Fascination with half-truths

In the tense polarity of the world, the fascination of evil has its roots in the exclusion of one pole of reality, in the deceitfulness of a half-truth which is taken to be the whole truth. Therefore the fascination of evil always indicates a neurotic rejection of parts of reality, repression, and 'suppressing the truth' (Rom. 1.18). Where this exclusion is not noticed, social groups and individuals can adopt fundamentalist half-truths and precisely in so doing think that they are 'simply' and 'surely' serving God. Fundamentalists are pious neurotics who suppress parts of the truth and then foist their own half-truths on God and the world. Half-truths could be felt to have a pleasant fascination. Whole truths are painful. Neurosis is the flight from the pain of the whole truth; it is the fascinating tyranny of evil half-truth. The tempter of Jesus can also call up fundamentalist half truths from scripture to put to him. A fundamentalist authoritarian insistence on part truths – loving God half-heartedly – frees destructive forces contrary to the facts, which burden the history of Christianity.

Half-love is an ideal betrayed. To love God with all one's heart means to accept the aggressive drive, 'the evil drive,' as Martin Buber calls it 'into love of God. The two drives unite, in other words provide the undirected potency of passion with a direction which makes it fit for great love and great service. Only in this way, and in no other, can the human being become whole.'[19]

2. Fascination through overestimating oneself

Religious communities have promised 'great and entire love' to their founders. But it is a universal experience that insistence on ideals can produce the precise opposite. The 'special way to perfection' can become a particularly imperfect way. Religions always also waged an underground war against the intentions of their founders. Crossing of self-imposed frontiers and breaking out of self-chosen forms is not just a consequence of a false estimation of oneself, but must also be seen in connection with the fascination of going beyond oneself, competitive rebellion against the 'fathers', and a childish joy at belatedly having grown up.

Christians are in particular danger, not only as individuals but also as church communities, where they want to be particularly virtuous. No holy scriptures, foundation documents or statutes protect them from this. With a minimum of self-criticism, any religious order will be able to note special mechanisms of suppression alongside heroic achievements in the specific realization of its charisma, for example under the ideological cloak of needs for innovation. Whether this is 'gnoseological concupiscence', to use Karl Rahner's phrase, or a guilty perversion, cannot be discussed here.

In this connection we have been concerned only with demonstrating a few background reasons why the claim to deliver from evil, both within Christianity and projected outside, can itself become evil, and why even now religious violence can deck itself with the fascinating aura of a 'religion' and 'loyal belief'.

VI. 'Demystification' of evil

God's work of dividing the primal chaos creates order, and separates light from darkness in the process of evolutionary creation. Despite the new creation in Christ (II Cor. 5.17), his eschatological work of division is preceded by an undecided history. The wisdom of meaningful life in an undecided world is codified in the parable of the wheat and the tares. Where we announce sole claims to be the true religion, the pure culture and the right policy, we insert ourselves hastily and destructively into God's eschatological work of division. Where we want to pull God's kingdom so to speak by the hair into history, we drive his spirit out of the world. The last things will then be worse than the first. In the conditions of an undecided history we must always accept a great mass of tares among the wheat (cf. Matt. 13.27ff.).

Here it is not a matter of favouring the enemy, but of that merciful hope which does not break the bruised reed and does not quench the flickering flax. It characterizes 'true religion' (cf. Isa. 42.3f.; Matt. 12.20). But because we have God's wisdom in earthen vessels, time and again we find that we do have not just the professionally pious, but also poor others and words of scripture, against us.

1. Counter-strategies

The fascination of evil as a fascination with half-truths of redemption glossed over with religious celebration, raises the question of counter-strategies which go beyond an enlightened tolerance. If the lofty claim to bring deliverance from evil is not to degenerate into collective feelings of guilt or hypocrisy, it can be maintained in Christianity only through shared rituals of remembrance and forgiveness and a constant revision of the psycho-social function of its models and paradigms which create meaning in history.

The overcoming of evil cannot be promised except against the horizon of history. Yet against this very horizon a goal appears beyond the contingency of evil: the restoration of the image of God in human beings, taken up into a universal new creation. This can make life meaningful. Evil comes from anxiety about a meaningless life and from making fetishes of things and people. The good is meaningful. Initiation rites among tribal peoples are usually ceremonies which bring about the overcoming of anxiety through scenarios of anxiety. Peace marches, pilgrimages of the landless and other rites which bring people together to protest against injustice and to call for more dignified living conditions are demonstrations which denounce the bloody sacrifice of life, strip the false aura of fatalism from evil, and work in a historically responsible way to overcome it.

2. Models

Models play a significant part in overcoming evil and unmasking its fascination. Therefore Christianity must urgently reflect on the role of its church fathers and saints. In the history of the churches they have often evoked violent images and actions, prejudices and unworldly passiveness, instead of being productive models of faith. The preaching of the church fathers on the Jews is not innocent of the persecution of Jews by Christians. In America, St James, the 'killer of the Moors', to whom appeal was made in the liberation struggle against the Muslim Moors, became the Indian-killer (*Mataindios*).

In Portuguese America, even before the battle of Lepanto in 1571, such victories of faith over the Indios were dedicated to 'Nossa Senhora da Vitoria' (Our Lady of Victory).[20] Clad in a white tunic and a golden king's robe, with a crown on her head and the palm of victory in her right hand, she is like the goddess Victoria erected by the emperor Gracian in the distant Forum Romanum. She no longer casts down the 'mighty' from their thrones, no longer exalts the 'lowly'. The first parish in Brazil, in Bahia do Salvador, bears her name.

3. De-demonizing of the others

The 'demystification' of evil by preaching love of neighbour and enemy is aimed at a general de-demonization of the others. For Christians, the other is neither enemy, rival or stranger. The others are the poor, the excluded and those on the periphery of society. Christianity promises the demystification of the magic of evil by a correction of social injustice, by the discovery of personal responsibility for evil, and by the assurance that in principle evil can be forgiven and that the roots of victory over it lie in Jesus Christ. He has promised all peoples deliverance from the need and humiliation of a damaged life.

He guarantees the excluded and the prisoners, the poor and the others, their irreplaceable individuality. In a universal covenant fellowship he encourages them – because redemption is near – to dedicate themselves to walking upright, with raised head, in a whole life.

Translated by John Bowden

Notes

1. In the early morning of 20 April 1997 five young middle-class people went past the Pataxó Indio Galdino Jesus dos Santos, who was sleeping on a bench at a bus stop in Brasilia. They suddenly decided to buy a can of fuel at the next petrol station, returned, poured it over Galdino and set light to him. When questioned by the police, they said, 'We just wanted to see him running away in flames. It was only a joke.'

2. Cf. Blumenkranz, *Die Judenpredigt Augustins*, Basel 1946.

3. Ambrose, *Epist.* 40, PL 16, 1104ff.

4. St Bernard, *Obras Completas*, Vol. 1, Madrid 1983, 503.

5. Cf. *Retractationes*, 1131, CSEL 36, 137.

6. *Summa theologiae* II^a II^x, q. 10 a. 8.

7. Cf. J. de Acosta, *De procuranda indorum salute* (1567), Madrid 1984 (CSIC), Book II,Ch. 12 (pp. 338, 341); Proemio (p. 69).

8. J. de Anchieta, *Obras Complecas*, Vol. 6, Cartas (ed. A. A. Viotti), Sâo Paulo [2]1984, 197 [letter of 14 April 1563].

9. Cf. Y. Congar, *'Ecce constitui te super gentes et regna* (Jer 1,10) in Geschichte und Gegenwart', in J. Auer and R. Volk (eds.), *Theologie in Geschichte und Gegenwart* (FS M. Schmaus), Munich 1957, 671–96.

10. *Acta Apostolicae Sedis* 34, 1942, 105–11.

11. Cf. B. Gantin, 'Valeurs universelles des religions traditionnelles africaines', *Pro Dialogo Bulletin*, 93, 1996/3, 318–27: 320.

12. Cf. R. Benedetti, 'Um Deus e Varios "deuses"', *Dialogo-Revista de Ensino Religioso* 7, August 1997, 33–9: 36.

13. B. Diaz del Castillo, *Historia verdadera de la conquista de la Nueva Espania*, 2 vols, Mexico 1980: Vol 1, 161ff.

14. Charlemagne's *Capitulatio de partibus Saxoniae* (782) gave the Saxons the same alternative as the so-called *Requerimiento* (1513) gave the Indios: conversion to Christianity or death.

15. A. Görres and K. Rahner, *Das Bose. Wege zu seiner Bewaltigung in Psychotherapie und Christentum*, Freiburg, Basel and Vienna 1982, 182.

16. Cf. R. Girard, *La violence et le sacré*, Paris 1972, passim.

17. A. Vieira, 'Sermâo decimo quarto' (1633), in *Sermôes*, Vol. 4, Torno 11, No. 6, 301.

18. L. Volk (ed), *Akten Kardinal Michael V. Faulhabers 1917–1945*, Vol. 26, Mainz 1978, 824 [13 November 1941] and 845 [17 November 1941].

19. M. Buber, *Bilder von Gut und Böse*, Heidelberg 1986, 35f.

20. Cf. N. B. Megale, *Invocacôes da Virgem Maria no Brasil*, Petrópolis 1997, 465–9.

Satan and Antichrist – Necessary Symbols?

Rosemary Muir Wright

The fascination of evil is most sharply focussed in the symbolic forms of Satan and the Antichrist, as metaphorical expressions of a malign power destructive of humanity. These entities have always been difficult to define because the inherent ambiguity of the concept of evil allowed for linguistic confusion and varieties of exegetical response. A powerful creative tradition which encompasses Milton's *Paradise Lost* and Michelangelo's *Last Judgment* in the Sistine Chapel ensures the continuing materialization of these agents of evil in physical form. As long as there is a visual entity, the concept of evil as epitomized in Satan, the Prince of Darkness', retains its power to fascinate and to haunt human intelligence. The very word 'satanic' suggests both attraction and repulsion, and it may be the seductive power of evil which ensures its continuing fascination.

I. Permanent fascination

At first sight the figures of Satan and the Antichrist appear to belong to the imagery and exegetical literature of the Middle Ages, but this is to underrate their potential.[1] The reappearance of such figures in the twentieth century has to be taken seriously in the shadow of the Holocaust and Hiroshima. Despite the fundamentalist wing and the various Christian sects of the 1970s and 1980s, there is discomfiture in the mainstream churches about the survival of the figure of Satan. There is even more unease about the symbol of the Antichrist. Journalism and the media, however, ensure that both figures are alive and well, especially in the activities of self-styled cults and the New Religious Movements like the Order of the Solar Temple, which was claimed to have killed a woman near its Montreal headquarters because they believed she had given birth to the Antichrist in 1994.

1. A cosmic and earthly force

The fascination with this theme is further demonstrated by the success of films like *The Omen* directed by Graham Baker, in which the character of the Antichrist is projected as a major world leader who controls global companies with huge economic potential. *The Omen* reveals this insidious challenge as something rooted in the very systems which operate political and economic control. Unlike the symbol of Satan, which tends to point to a cosmic source, the figure of Antichrist is recurrent in history. The fundamentalist fringes of modern Christianity would assert the reality of this evil on the basis of scriptural truth. Even the entertainment value of such Hammer films as *The Devil Rides Out*, 1967, not only perpetuates the traditional myths of Satan but induces in even the most sceptical audience a sense of being on guard against the seductive intrusion of this form of evil.

However, if we are to analyse the fascination of these two figures, we need to establish a fundamental distinction between Satan and the Antichrist. The symbol of the Antichrist allows humanity to give the Devil a face and a human form, while preserving the adopted distinction between spiritual and moral evil. Satan can be relegated to the spiritual world and possibly emasculated, while the Antichrist is seen as the earthly progeny of that cosmic force, albeit under the ultimate control.

2. The New Testament in the contemporary context

The fascination with the man of evil alluded to in the New Testament has always been fuelled by specific historical and social conditions, from the earliest visual representations in mediaeval Spanish manuscripts to the film character of Damian Thorn. The current fascination with evil at least opens up the debate and pitches it into a contemporary context, especially relevant to the last fifty years, in which the figure of the Antichrist has been seen to walk abroad in the guise of Hitler or Saddam Hussein, while the hysteria of satanic abuse has cast a shadow over the history of those professions most geared to protect the innocent and the marginalized. The continuing fascination with the symbolism of evil indicates that in certain circumstances, evil calls forth a guaranteed response. While the imagery of Satan instinctively repels, the image of the Antichrist is designed to make evil attractive because of his rewards proffered in exchange for allegiance. His personality can be seen to command a particular fascination.

People are drawn to follow him, attracted by his physical presence and seduced by his words. Yet although he preys on human weakness, he himself is seen to be remote from this. Despite the Christian bias of these symbols, the life force of the satanic lies outside the world of religion, and it is this which makes it so dangerous because in the twentieth century Satan lies beyond the control of a prevailing belief. The label is easy to apply to marginalize and demonize the 'enemy'. Because of the ambiguity about the purpose of evil in the world and the interpretation of the texts which set out the role models of the Antichrist and the Devil, the twentieth-century fascination may be the result of imperfect knowledge of the sources of these ideas and their manipulative potential.

II. Antichrist in history

In this article, I will concentrate on the less familiar imagery of the Antichrist. The destructive horrors of modern war and its control, the brutalization of human beings and the obsession with material securities, all provide a climate in which the reality of a power base such as that which Antichrist was said to command could seem dangerously potent. What is forgotten is that this form of evil, however absolute for a time, heralded the coming of the messianic kingdom. The birth of the Antichrist signalled the return of Christ to the world.

Whether we believe in the historical reality of this figure or whether we understand it as a symbol for an evil that is sensed to be existent in the world, the figure of the Antichrist can adapt its human form to suit any political reality. In exegesis, the nature of the Antichrist was both recognizable and disguised. It is in this inherent paradox that the fascination of the figure lies, exercising a persistent, even haunting influence on our imaginations.

1. Cosmic struggle (the book of Revelation)

Visual imagery, in conjunction with the written sources, created a set of expectations for the figure of the Antichrist, many of which are still in place. The key text which has provided so much of the imagery of the cosmic battle between good and evil at the end of the world is the book of Revelation. New Testament references to the 'prince of darkness' and the 'son of perdition' found visionary expansion in chapter 13, where the seven-headed beast which arose from the sea was identified as the Antichrist, the persecutor of the church on earth and the agent of Satan as the leader of all the evil forces abroad in the world. As the book of Revelation was a type of literary work known as apocalypse, it dealt with eschatology or the events of the end of the world, revealed in a series of majestic visions.[2]

The text calls on its readers to resist the forces of evil which oppose the working out of God's plan for the world and Christ's work in the establishment of his kingdom on earth. It is a book about struggle, both the cosmic struggle with the forces of evil and the personal contest of every individual. In this contest, Antichrist is the key protagonist, for as the agent and incarnation of Satan, he represents the devil in the world. Men were forced to worship an image of the Antichrist on pain of death and to receive the mark of the devil on their right hand and forehead before they could engage in the traffic of earthly goods. The text of Revelation is completely theocentric, revealing a series of visions the symbolism of which is not fixed but constantly capable of reinterpretation. Implicit in the text is the demand on the listener or reader to respond, and it is this power to provoke response which has rendered the book of Revelation so susceptible to contemporary resonances.

2. Malice and iniquity (tenth century)

A body of legendary material also ensured the continuing interest in the Antichrist figure. One such was the famous account written by Adso, Abbot of Montier-en-Der, in the mid-tenth century, which represented a summary of the traditional material.

> Antichrist, who, though he be a man, nevertheless will be the source of all sins, and the *son of perdition*, that is, the son of the devil, not through nature, but through imitation, because he will carry out the devil's will in all things; because the fullness of diabolical power and of depraved nature will dwell bodily in him, where there will be hidden away all the treasures of malice and iniquity.[3]

Another source of information was the letter of Pseudo-Methodius, which described the coming of the Antichrist from the East, being born of the tribe of Dan. This was a fruitful text for the demonization of the Jews in the later Middle Ages and beyond.

If we were to examine the contexts in which the imagery of the Antichrist were most prevalent, we might learn something of the circumstances in which the fascination with evil gains a secure hold. The first verifiable appearance of Antichrist as a man appears in Spain in the tenth century, at a time of doctrinal controversy in association with a new commentary on the Apocalypse which may have drawn on an early Christian source like Irenaeus in *Against Heresies*.

. . . he (Antichrist) being endued with all the power of the devil, shall come, not as a righteous king, nor as a legitimate king in subjection to God, but as an impious, unjust and lawless one; as an apostate, iniquitous and murderous; as a robber, concentrating in himself satanic apostasy and setting aside idols to persuade men that he himself is God, raising up himself as the only idol, having in himself the multifarious errors of other idols.[4]

The implication that the threat to the church will come from a man has had a continuing hold on the imagination, especially as the texts stressed his duplicity. The Branch Davidian sect under David Koresh, whose members were prepared to die in the flames of Waco, and the 900 followers of Jim Jones at the People's Temple in Guyana who took cyanide at his request, would find their mediaeval equivalents.

3. Subversive society (eleventh century)

Another aspect of the Antichrist theme is in the association of this figure with the politics of the Middle East, evident as early as the First Crusade and the recovery of Jerusalem in the latter years of the eleventh century. The legend of the Antichrist had described how he would make his way to Jerusalem and sit in the temple of God as if he were God himself. This legend was linked with another, that of the Last Emperor, who would regain Jerusalem for Christ, reigning there for a period before laying down his crown on the Mount of Olives in token of the predicted appearance of the Antichrist. It would be easy to see contemporary equivalence in a powerful political figure challenged by the church on the soil of Jerusalem itself. The restitution of Jerusalem to the Jews or the easing of the tensions of the Middle East from the threat of Moslem fundamentalists could be made to carry apocalyptic overtones. Again, contests of powers, the shadow of heresy and the threat to political authority could all conjure up the spectre of the Antichrist, who could be made to stand as the ultimate enemy for whatever cause seeking an eschatological outcome.

One of the contexts in which he can generate support is his appeal to the marginalized, the misfits of society in whom he sparks an energizing sense of rebellion which is self-destructive. His mediaeval followers are pictured in the illustrated Apocalypse cycles as including the poor, the outcast and the beggar, the malformed and the adolescent. To them he offers the prospect of a change of circumstance, a restoration into a new society which will wreak vengeance on the one which had so misused them. The spectre of a subversive society within society once raised by groups like the Cathars, the Gnostics and the Freemasons lives on in attitudes to the

1960s satanist cults and the New Ageism of the 1980s. The church under threat, the trials of the present time, the ultimate failure of the Antichrist against the people of God, these were themes of immense propaganda value.

4. A false church (thirteenth century)

The Middle Ages completely understood the dual role of the Antichrist as an external force threatening the church and as an operator working on the internal disposition of fallen humanity. As in certain contemporary contexts, the mediaeval promotion of a concrete figure of evil was the work of the orthodox, *conservative forces in the church*. The lavishly illustrated Moralized Bibles of the thirteenth century had much to say about the Antichrist and his historical predecessors, by demonstrating how the true church faced a new enemy in the form of a false church which claimed allegiance through false teaching, false prophecy and exclusion. Challenges to orthodoxy have been a fruitful context for the fermentation of ideas of the Antichrist. For the mediaeval audience of these books the devil was not just a symbolic entity but a force working in the world, penetrating human nature to form a dark side especially prevalent in those who exercise power.

In some pictures, human figures are shadowed by demonic forms, especially the figures of the Jews, who were identified in the company of Antichrist and revealed as his agents. In images addressed primarily to the clergy, Antichrist was distinguished by the unmistakable evidence of his own monstrosity in bearing three faces under a huge horned crown in parody of the divine Trinity, which represented the unity of all goodness. This opened the way to link the political abuse of power with its spiritual abuse. In many of the Apocalypse cycles the artist stressed Antichrist's aspiration to be as God by giving him all the power and allure of an angelic creation. His physical state was one of vigour, even sexuality. This *sexual magnetism* continues to be associated with the Antichrist and provides one of the strongest reasons for his fascination. In some ways this may have stemmed from the belief in the bestial nature of the Satan, who was believed to indulge in uncontrollable sexual appetites. The consequence was the witch-craze, with its senseless burnings of the emotionally and psychologically vulnerable.

The tragic ease with which this tag could be used to get rid of the socially undesirable is not unfamiliar to the *racial prejudice* of the twentieth century. The most obvious recurrence is the old fear of satanic ritual abuse in both America and in Europe, where in a troubled society, culture can find an external demon to provide an explanation and a vindication for fundamentalist crusades.[5] Survivor stories, like Lauren Stratford's *Satan's Underground*, encouraged the belief that the Devil was real and alive, a hysteria which only died down after the publication of Professor La Fontaine's report in 1994, *The Extent and Nature of Organized Ritual Abuse*. She reported that such disturbances had been caused by a complex context of mental illness, child neglect and bad housing, and claimed that the conviction of belief in evil cults stems from the powerful cultural axioms on which it draws.

5. The pope as Antichrist (fifteenth century)

The idea that the Antichrist would be a person of immense political power was well established by the fifteenth century, when he was consistently represented as a royal personage, surrounded by a retinue and identified with treachery, material luxury and the control of wealth. However, the late Middle Ages saw a new development in the interpretation of the Antichrist as a false preacher, especially as the accusations of imperial polemics had acquired a new specificity in claiming that the Antichrist would come as a pope. The fifteenth century Savoy Apocalypse (Madrid, Biblioteca de El Escorial, Cod.MS Vitrina, I), for all its chivalric tone carries a dark message within its illustrations, signalled by the baleful yellow eyes of the Devil and the fanatic preaching of the Antichrist from his pulpit. The pessimism of its context is marked in the shift in representation from a tyrannical king to a haunting hooded presence in the form of a preacher of malign influence.[6] This was a challenge to the church from within its own ranks. The power of the Antichrist depicted in that manuscript made for Amadeus of Savoy is that of a being electrified by his mission and charged by an intensity which brooks evil. This demagogic power is to be seen in the block books and the propaganda images of the Reformation and beyond, for with the intervention of Luther, the whole context changed, as the Antichrist was then identified with the papacy itself.

III. Power and oppression

In the circumstances of the twentieth century, the lure of these legends has re-entered visual consciousness, magnified by the mass media and empowered by very similar circumstances of power-struggle and oppression. Evil still preys on the emotionally damaged, the maladjusted and the neurotic. The appeal of the cinematic representation might seem to lie in the vicarious safety of the cinema, where the audience can look on evil and remain untouched, but the public warnings about films like the *Exorcist*,

1973, and the help-groups set up to cope with the filmgoers, suggest that the effects of such films on the vulnerable were disturbing.

1. *Renewed force*

The sustained evidence of belief in a force of evil in the world cannot be ignored, despite our attempts to explain it in psychological or scientific terms. If we were to be sceptical of the figure of Satan as something formed by 'the eye of childhood', we might be less dismissive of the figure of Antichrist. The latter representation is much more likely to convince because the Antichrist is seen as moving among mankind in the guise of someone well-known, charismatic and authoritative. Those who might suspect something other are silenced or endangered. As the Devil comes to be mentioned less and less in mainstream Christianity and relegated to the side lines as an embarrassing entity, so the concept of evil channelled into a single human being may take on renewed force.

2. *Warning symbols*

If we accept that these figures have taken on life from the rich literary and visual tradition by which evil is given concrete form, we are still faced with the uneasy possibility that the warning which they embody is real. Once we perceive that these symbols are a warning, then we have a genuine need of their retention, because by that recognition we are called on to make a choice. That choice could be a liberating force and a determining element in our resistance to corruption on the grand scale. We may need to hold on to these symbols to refine our alertness to the abuse of power, to the treachery of words and to the predatory nature of wealth. Satan and his son will always stand out of range, so there is little point in debating their reality except as a concept of moral evil, but there is every point in their retention as signs in the many-voiced communication of the twentieth century. As evil is so often surreptitious and suggestive, there is justification in prayer.

> Because most of us have been graced by an almost instinctive sense of horror at the outrageousness of evil, when we recognize its presence, our own personalities are honed by the awareness of its existence.[7]

We need not simply resign ourselves, for our freedom depends on our continuing to exercise our choice to resist throughout the entire span of our living existence. The warning posed by the symbol of Satan instantly reminds us of our capacity to choose. And it is this which makes us free to choose again. In that choice lies the hope of humanity that individuals will always resist the suggestive power of anything which is not creative and life-giving, whether it be a hostile intelligence or the harmful destructive tendencies of human nature.

Notes

1. B. McGinn, 'Portraying Antichrist in the Middle Ages', in *The Use and Abuse of Eschatology, Mediaevalia Lovaniensia*, Series I/Studia XV, 1988, 1–48.

2. R. Bauckham, *The Theology of the Book of Revelation*, Cambridge 1998, 164.

3. B. McGinn, *Visions of the End: Apocalyptic Traditions in the Middle Ages*, New York 1979, 107; Adso of Montier-en-der, *De Ortu et Tempore Antichristi*, ed. D. Verhelst, Turnholt 1676, 6–16.

4. J. Poesch, *Antichrist Imagery in Anglo-French Apocalypse Manuscripts*, PhD thesis, University of Pennsylvania Fine Arts, Ann Arbor 1966, 24.

5. P. Stanford, *The Devil. A Biography*, reprinted London 1997, 252–7.

6. R. Muir Wright, *Art and Antichrist in Mediaeval Europe*, Manchester 1995, 162.

7. M. Scott Peck, *The Road Less Travelled*, reprinted London 1990, 299.

The Attraction of Apocalypse and the Evil of the End

Catherine Keller

The most satisfying kind of evil can be found in murder mysteries. I love them: the villain is irredeemable but smart, the wrong unpardonable but fascinating, the detective work guaranteed to succeed in the end, when justice is done, the evil excised, and the pieces of normal life fall neatly back into place. Not only does such a story satisfy our curiosity about evil, it limits its impact to something that can be solved: the complexity that held our interest reduces in the end to a reassuring simplicity. But there is another kind and scope of what we encode as evil that defies such narrative closure. In the end, even if evil is defeated, the pieces cannot fall back into place. For this evil has shattered the world itself.

I. World-shattering evil

This article suggests that the sort of destruction which brings down a world – a people, a culture, an ecosphere – has inspired the narratives of apocalypse. These narratives manage the unmanageable: they turn collective despair into communal hope. Indeed, they transmute horror into fascination and annihilation into solution. Because we stand at the end of a century of genocide and ecocide, indeed, at the announced 'end' of a modernity predicated upon world-annihilation in the name of progress, it behoves us to meditate upon the attraction of apocalypse: as a story of salvation from, but perhaps also attraction to, world-destruction.

Christian practice has tended to focus on the former, more manageable kind of evil: that is, on personal sins, which the church can detect and correct. 'Original sin', a doctrine capable of articulating the systemic character of evil, tends to be reduced to a myth of the first personal transgression and an explanation for all subsequent ones. Furthermore, like a murder mystery, we know in advance that the case will be solved, not by detection but by atonement. Christianity has allowed us to face, indeed to obsess about, our own private sins or those of our neighbours. But it has kept the other kind of evil, the systemic, world-shattering kind, at the edge of its awareness. Despite the canonization of John's Apocalypse as the end of the Christian meta-narrative, mainstream forms of Christianity have had uneasy relations with apocalypticism. Augustine lashed out at the chiliasts of his day for their 'superficial, literal' reading.[1] And Luther, despite 'sola scriptura', declared that 'my spirit cannot accommodate itself to this book' because 'Christ is neither taught nor known in it'.[2]

Theologically speaking, we are left with a mystery of our own: why did Christianity marginalize its apocalyptic tradition? Did that tradition provide a narrative with healing and saving power? Can it now? 'Apocalypse', after all, does not mean annihilation, but revelation: 'disclosure, unveiling'. Yet the narrative has been used as a theodicy with which both to face and to justify annihilation. The mythic dramatization of the final confrontation of good and evil, with the destruction of most life on the planet as 'collateral damage', may constrain, or may inspire, human agents of world-extermination. The mystery darkens . . . Does the ancient vision of the end of the world effect a self-fulfilling prophecy?

Clearly the Apocalypse provides a mythological nest for groups past and current that stimulate our pity, curiosity and consternation – but hardly our identification. The subject of theology, however, is not primarily the Other as interesting object of study but the self as inter-subjective agent. So we might ask: might the apocalyptic pattern also function as a subliminal cultural habit among the rest of us, those whose Christianity may involve no end-of-the-world piety? Do we also respond with deep, mythically preformed reflexes to what we perceive as world-threatening evil? The mystery becomes more complex as it becomes more honest, more self-implicating – and as I will suggest 'in the end', may precisely hinge on a marginal spirituality of complexity itself.

II. Hoping for a new creation (messianism)

The most common form of modern apocalypticism took off like wildfire in mid-nineteenth century America: a 'premillennialist' Protestantism which in the early twentieth century would theologically frame 'fundamentalism'. These Christians developed an intricate historiography of seven 'dispensations'. We are approaching the last, the 'millennium', and may expect during our lifetimes the return of Jesus 'upon the clouds'; if we have been 'born again' we will be 'raptured' up bodily to meet him and the 'saved'

dead, with whom we will look down upon the spectacle of earth falling to
pieces through some timely combination of military, nuclear, social and
ecological mayhem. We will then be granted new bodies and élite status in
the coming theocracy, in which Jesus and the saints reign from Jerusalem
until the final judgment and resurrection.[3]

1. The earth will be purged

Consider, however, a group known as Heaven's Gate. Famous for the
suicide of its thirty-nine members on Good Friday 1997, they were avid
Bible readers who considered the churches moribund. Their original
leaders, 'Do' and 'Ti', identified themselves as the two witnesses of
Rev. 11.3. The thirty-nine went on video to record their happiness at
leaving their earthly 'vehicles' behind on the corrupt earth, to join a space
ship hidden in the tail of the comet Hale-Bopp. Having thus narrowly
escaped the imminent 'recycling' of planet Earth, they will receive higher,
sexless bodies in the heavens.

Premillennialist Christians, who abhor such New Age/Christian syn-
cretism, nonetheless share with them a pattern of belief: the earth, doomed
by its own wickedness, will soon be radically purged; social reform is
futile. One can convert only individuals, who through obedience can win
through to the triumphant end, controlled by Omnipotence working
through various higher beings from the heavens. This is truly faith as flight
– indeed, in both cases as literal ascent to the skies – from the immanent
catastrophe. Such apocalypse catalyzes great personal transformation and
communal cohesiveness, even while it breeds social quietism in the face of
the besetting evils.

Yet such passivity is not apolitical, as the case of the 'new religious Right'
of the Reagan 1980s demonstrates. By identifying evil as supernatural
Satan whose historical manifestations are the Beasts of communism, New
Age and feminism, and Armageddon as thermonuclear exchange, fundamentalist ideologues wrought of a once non-voting constituency an
astoundingly activist opposition to moral liberalism and social justice.[4]
Imported to Latin America, it evinces growing success in overwhelming a
liberation-tainted Roman Catholicism and accommodating the interests of
the US-based global economy.

2. The 'new creation' of Cristobal

Unknown to most, however, its genetic code dates back to the origins of
modernity in the conquest of America. Cristobal Colon, aka Columbus,
equated his 'discovery' of the 'new world' with the *apokalypsis* of the 'new
creation'. Thus he wrote in 1500: 'Of the New Heaven and Earth which

our Lord made, as St John writes in the Apocalypse . . . he made me the messenger thereof and showed me where to go.'[5] Such subliminal messianism seems to have sanctified the colon/izing efforts of Europe and then the United States, whatever divergent theologies the missionaries who accompanied the conquerors and traders were preaching. It justified a biblical scale of genocide and ecocide against the indigenous populations. Those of us who benefit from so-called free markets (if the enforced dependency of a deprived majority is 'free') may need to recognize our colusion with this 'crypto-apocalypse'. Tracing its secular effects begins to link the Euro-American mainstream to the overtly apocalyptic Right.

III. Prophetic heritage

But the mystery is not thereby solved. There are radically other ways of interpreting the apocalypse as sacred narrative: i.e., the voices of liberation theology, in which a powerful tradition of biblical exegesis from and for the oppressed community has reclaimed the Apocalypse.[6]

1. Liberation theology

They would situate evil fully within history, and locate its most dangerous manifestation in precisely the systemic structures of oppression erected by Western colonialism and ultra-modernized by the global marketplace. With considerable support from New Testament scholarship they can read John's cryptic letter as an anti-imperialist allegory.[7] Revelation 17–19 details the fall of Babylon, code for Rome, precisely in terms of the collapse of the economic superstructure of client kings, merchants and sea captains. 'For your merchants were the great men of the earth, and all nations were deceived by your sorcery. And in her was found the blood of prophets and of saints, and of all who have been slain on earth' (18.24f.). Relevant? The breaking of the seals, the blowing of the trumpets, the whole mythopoeic vortex of socio-ecological cataclysm, need not then be read as God's punitive will: for liberationists, they signify the way in which the known world has been gripped by the Beast – Rome then, the First World now, such that it strips bare its environment, devours its own non-renewable resources, undermines its own stability. In a misogynist but precise symbolism, the Beast strips and consumes his own Whore-Queen (17.16).

Judgment is needed. But the 'destruction of the destroyers of the earth' (11.18) is not read by liberationists as a warrant for vengeance. Rather, it signals a hope that a sustainable justice will be achieved, in which there will be 'water of life without payment' (21.5), a nourishing environment of (replanted) trees. Not an ahistorical closure for the earth,[8] not the supernatural heaven into which Augustine translated the 'new skies and new earth', but rather a 'healing of the nations' (22.2) is anticipated. Thus the entire text can be read as a liberation manifesto: evil collapses upon itself, devastating the poor and the rich alike (6.15). However, its God does not heap evil upon evil, but dis/closes a space for the utopian possibility.

It would naturally be anachronistic to find there a call to revolution or even institutional change: apocalypse grows from a prophetic eschatological tradition in which social analysis, if it can be called such, was inscribed in a densely spiritual, politically intuitive, and by necessity underground code. The history of apocalyptic effects is deeply embedded in all subsequent social utopias and revolutions in the West, as the socialist philosopher Ernst Bloch has demonstrated.[9] The translations of revelation into revolution become especially apparent in the radical Reformation. But the millennialist utopia and the bloodshed which precedes it have effectively secularized themselves in the bourgeois and Marxist revolutions.[10]

2. Anti-apocalypse

The difference between the above contemporary deployments of apocalypse is not just political, but hermeneutical: so we might distinguish between a 'retro-apocalypse', which seeks to identify its own current situation as the moment which John prophesied, and thus obliterates the difference between the biblical and the current context; and on the other a 'neo-apocalypse', which emphasizes the importance of the social, economic and political relations formative of the biblical context and our own. If, as Boesak argues, those 'who do not struggle together with God's people for the sake of the gospel, and who do not feel in their own bodies the meaning of oppression and the freedom and joy of fighting against it shall have grave difficulty understanding this letter from Patmos' (38), then any merely anti-apocalyptic stance must reveal itself as anti-revolutionary.

So we must acknowledge that in mainline Christendom's quiet 'anti-apocalypse' lies not just abhorrence of enthusiasts, but also the institutional will to self-conservation. Indeed as soon as Constantine undertook the Christianization of that very empire coded by John as Babylon, the church lost interest in any end of this world. It identified the thousand-year kingdom with the church triumphant on the earth. And not for nearly a millennium did the Joachimite utopian idea of a new and improved age in history reappear. When it did, it unleashed a whole tradition of critique of the Roman pontiff as 'Whore of Babylon', culminating in the Reformation.

But when the Protestant form became a state-sponsored institution, it drew upon the princes to eradicate its own radical wing, the Anabaptists of Thomas Muntzer, who hooked Joachimite apocalypse to the Peasant Revolt and began to name Luther adjunct Antichrist.

3. The challenge

Nonetheless, liberation theology and other contextual theologies – such as the feminist theology in which my work is noted – seem to me most capable of evolution into the third millennium only as they outgrow their own simplistic, *dualistic tendencies*: to demonization of the other (capitalist, white, male) and to 'identity politics' (of class, race or gender).[11] Does this mean one must urge apocalypse-patterned movements to abandon apocalyptic rhetorical strategies?

I think not. However much we may want to challenge the morality of any revolutionary violence, messianic purge, construal of opponent as demon, Christians who internalize the prophetic heritage of liberation from social oppression who stand with Jesus the student of Isaiah and of John the Baptist, cannot merely negate the apocalypse pattern. Indeed by definition we *cannot* purge our traditions of apocalypse without yielding to it: should we demonize demonizers? Note for instance how Augustine's anti-apocalyptic stance did not prevent him from the cruelty of the penultimate chapter of *The City of God*, a grotesque literalization of apocalyptic mythemes of damnation; nor did Luther's anti-apocalypse prevent him from identifying the Pope or Turk as Antichrist, at his convenience.

IV. Counter-apocalypse

If neither a naive pro-apocalypse nor an outright anti-apocalypse seem theologically inviting, where does this leave us? Does the mystery turn out to be mere irrationality, silence, double-negation? Do we find ourselves either incapable of a transforming commitment in the face of world-threatening evils or not tempted to the potentially violent or suicidal call of unmitigated apocalypse? Are we then doomed to rerun the church's increasingly ineffectual mix of self-serving institutionalism and legitimate caution?

1. No simplistic dualism

Perhaps. But consciousness (etymologically 'knowing-together') may allow us, in community, to 'fold together' (*com-plicare*) our contradictory options. Let us then consider the dialectical alternative of a '*counter-apocalypse*'. This counters the simplistic dualism of good v. evil to which the last biblical book has given rise; it counteracts the notion that there could be an end of time or a final solution to human struggle. There can only be shifts, transmutations, translations of history, degrading or evolutionary. If humans commit species suicide, nature's evolving history will not thereby cease to respond to the lure of God. A counter-apocalypse requires an irreversible and yet helical, rhythmic temporality – not deferred until the non-biblical eternity arrives but rather engaging us now, as we are willing, able, open.

Counter-apocalypse derives its biblical warrant less from John's Revelation than from the Isaianic and wisdom traditions as fulfilled in the life of the Jewish Jesus, whom we also read as a revealer of counter-apocalypse. The subtlety, irony and gradualism of the Gospel parables suggest that Jesus respected John the Baptist's fiery apocalypse of terminal good v. evil, but on better days imagined the realm of God as mustard seeds growing into stubborn weedy bushes, women kneading the yeast, lost sheep and lost coins showing up.[12]

Not surprisingly, the Gospels show little evidence of the sexism which was established by Pauline apocalyptic hierarchy as well as Johannine warrior messianism. In the latter, the 144,000-man martyr elite 'have not defiled themselves with women' (14.4), and the favoured image of evil is 'whore'. The only historic female referenced is 'Jezebel', and the imagery surrounding the Great City, the Evil Queen, is nearly pornographic in its power of fascination. The allegorical mother and virgin-bride figures hardly alleviate the force-field of ascetic male resentment. The monosexual hierarchy of masculine God-images and God-representatives is a symptom of the oversimplification that reflective Christians are in the process of outgrowing – without thereby apocalyptically fantasizing a cosmos purified of masculinity.

2. Relativizing revelation

As apocalyptic eschatology cannot be neatly purged from prophetic eschatology, so counter-apocalypse recognizes in itself a self-critical mode of apocalypse. It pursues no salvation through annihilation, but does confront evil, when necessary, with the dramatic metaphors of a global struggle against the voracity of the Beast, in which the future, indeed the salvation, of the earth is imminently at stake. Given the rush of capital to destroy not only multiple human worlds but the ecosphere which sustains all human worlds, the end of our millennium renders a certain apocalyptic sense of fury and hope indispensable. So counter-apocalypse affirms liberationist neo-apocalyptic attempts to interpret the text redemptively. But it also relativizes Revelation. It hears there a voice so abused by the beast as to tend – like most victims – to repeat the abusive pattern. This occurs through gross dualism, which must continually create new victims, and through unquestioned sexism, which feeds off the worst energies of the archetypal warrior-hero, signifying evil in female sex and power. Moral dualism operates through a fascination with its own objectified, exoticized, eroticized and readily demonized 'other'.

The God of simplistic good/evil codes is a caricature of the biblical deity. And perhaps 'his' demand for 'obedience' serves the secret purpose of continuously engendering new defiance. The apocalyptic rebellion of the angels must ever resonate with the adolescent in us all – and perhaps doom all patriarchal theology to a boring heaven, with the rebels expelled. If the fascination with evil transmutes our enemies into demons, thus perpetuating rather than untangling oppression, perhaps we need a substitute fascination, not just more prohibitions – and more rebellion.

3. The spirit of the edge

Perhaps something of what renders evil so interesting, what emanates from the pandemonium of the Apocalypse, appeals less to our repressed sinfulness than to our unintegrated need for complexity: for states of heightened, unsettling contrast. The God of the counter-apocalyptic eschatology appears here as the Spirit of the edge, the eschaton, where as the emerging sciences of chaos and complexity suggest, natural and social evolution take place. That eschaton is not a barrier, not an end, not a rigid boundary, but rather 'the edge of chaos': 'balance point', 'where the components of a system never quite lock into place, and yet never quite dissolve into turbulence, either'.[13]

Could the church become a site not for submission to numbing oversimplifications, but for exploration of that edge? Might we find our intensity, adventure, fascination precisely there – where chaos, the *tehom* of all genesis, gives rise to subtler forms of order? In this eschatological zone, the Spirit itself – not 'evil' – fascinates, provoking us to resist the tedious production of unnecessary suffering and drudgery, of human, religious and biological monocultures. This Spirit calls not through a tired rhetoric of final righteousness, but through the intimate sources of our own vitality.

Counter-apocalypse therefore must create its own postmodern collage of multiply interpreted, midrash-like, traditions. A complex reading of the text supports a reading of life as continuous evolution of spontaneous diversity. Unlike a detective novel, unlike any narrative of final solution, there is, thank God, no end to the mystery dis/closed at the edge.

Notes

1. Augustine, *The City of God* II, 20,21, trans. Henry Bettenson, Harmondsworth 1972, 1984, 940.

2. Martin Luther, 'Vorrede auf die Offenbarung S. Johannis' (1 522), *WA* VII, 404. English translation in *LW* 35, 398–9.

3. For a sensitive, psychohistorical account of contemporary apocalypticisms, see Charles B. Strozier, *Apocalypse: On the Psychology of Fundamentalism in America*, Boston 1994.

4. I.e. Hal Lindsey, *The Late Great Planet Earth*, New York 1973; Pat Robertson, Texe Marrs, etc.

5. Letter to Torres, *Journals and Other Documents on the Life and Voyages of Christopher Columbus*, trans. Samuel Eliot Morison, New York 1963, 291. See also Kirkpatrick Sale, *The Conquest of Paradise: Christopher Columbus and the Columbian Legacy*, New York 1990.

6. Allan A. Boesak, *Comfort and Protest: The Apocalypse from a South African Perspective*, Philadelphia 1987; Elisabeth Schüssler Fiorenza, *The Book of Revelation: Justice and Judgment*, Philadelphia 1985; Pablo Richard, *Apocalypse: A People's Commentary on the Book of Revelation*, Maryknoll, NY 1995.

7. Cf. for example Richard Horsley, *Jesus and the Spiral of Violence: Popular Jewish Resistance in Roman Palestine*, San Francisco 1987.

8. Unfortunately replicated by Jurgen Moltmann in his otherwise magisterial neo-apocalypse, *The Coming of God*, London and Minneapolis 1996.

9. Ernst Bloch, *The Principle of Hope* (1959), Vol. 2, Oxford and Cambridge, Mass. 1986.

10. Norman Cohn, *The Pursuit of the Millennium*, London and New York 1957.

11. I make this case in depth in *Apocalypse Now and Then: A Feminist Guide to the End of the World*, Boston 1996, from which much of the present argument is drawn.

12. John Dominic Crossan, *The Historical Jesus: The Life of a Mediterranean Jewish Peasant*, San Francisco and Edinburgh 1991, 227–51.

13. M. Mitchell Waldrop, *Complexity: The Emerging Science at the Edge of Order and Chaos*, New York 1992, 12.

The Mystery of Evil and the Hiddenness of God. Some Thoughts on Simone Weil

Alexander Nava

Upon first glance the suggeston that evil is somehow fascinating appears odd and dangerous. Might not a fascination with evil lead to an indulgence or delight in the suffering of others? Is a fascination with evil nothing but a pernicious voyeurism? Indeed, it is difficult to see how the destruction of persons and whole peoples in events such as the Spanish Conquest of the 'New World' or the Holocaust can be anything but repulsive. The portrayal of terrifying and iniquitous events in history as 'fascinating' may only indulge our fears and griefs, while stifling any hope of resistance in the face of evil. Perhaps this danger is, in part, what led Plato to ban the tragic poets from his Republic: the depiction of suffering and disaster by tragic drama brings pleasure to the audience in watching the actors lament and suffer. For Plato, such an emotional indulgence in the misery of others may undermine the pursuit of a just and virtuous life. The love of Truth, Justice, the Good is thereby displaced by a preoccupation with an emotional catharsis. A complacent and self-centred fascination with evil reigns over the life of virtue.

I. Struggle with the hidden God

In another vein, however, a fascination with evil may be less problematic. If it is possible to consider a fascination with evil in terms of an honest awareness of the nocturnal and harsh face of human existence, then a preoccupation with the question of evil may be the pathway to a more authentic and responsible Christian life. Such an awareness or attention to the fact that there is something fundamentally awry in history and society is, to be sure, at the heart of the Christian belief in 'original sin'. Contrary to optimistic and romantic portrayals of the human condition, Christianity insists that history and nature has been fractured and distorted by the effects of the Fall. The violence, suffering and terror of history makes obvious the fallen nature of human life. Whether or not, however, one can simply reduce the reality of evil to the effects of the Fall (and thus human sin) is a question at the heart of the so-called problem of evil. In the Jewish and Christian traditions, the presence of evil and suffering in history is, in fact, often related to human rebellion and sin. Nevertheless, there is also an important trajectory in the Jewish and Christian tradition which boldly struggles in the face of the omnipotence and omnibenevolence of God in a manner that refuses to reduce the presence of evil to human sin. In many different forms, this tradition expresses fear, terror and hope in what it names the 'hidden God'. As this article hopes to show, an awareness of or fascination with evil is related to a struggle with the hidden God. In the thought of Simone Weil, attention to divine hiddenness is joined with a tragic vision of the presence of force, violence and oppression in history and society. For Weil, such a tragic vision of history demands a response of compassion and justice in a manner that silences rational explanations for the problem of evil.

1. The reality of global suffering

In the light of the terrifying presence of affliction and evil in history and nature, the question of God's hiddenness confronts theology with an unavoidable urgency. The reality of evil can only be evaded at the price of theological dishonesty or complacency in the face of unjust suffering. Religion becomes no more than a consoling opiate when the dark face of existence is disregarded. Perhaps even more damaging in this regard, however, would be the suspicion of a failure of theology to interpret adequately a central symbol of Christianity, namely the cross. Such a theological failure would hold for the interpretation of the Hebrew Bible as well, especially the Psalms, Job, Lamentations, and the prophets. In these texts, an interpretation of the God who hides himself irrepressibly emerges from the experience of Israel's oppression and suffering. God appears to be absent from the struggles and cries of the afflicted.[1] A reading of God's hiddenness arises, then, both from the experiences of affliction and evil in human life on the one hand, and from the scriptures of Jews and Christians themselves on the other.

Liberation theology is one form of contemporary thought which creatively and honestly faces the reality of global suffering and oppression in relation to the hiddenness of God. Reflection on God is interpreted in the light of the struggles of the excluded, marginalized and colonized peoples, especially of the 'Third World'. The impact of power and violence in history and society (as in colonialism) receives thoughtful attention by such liberation thinkers. For Christian liberation theologians, the manifestation of God in history and society is located where God is most seemingy absent: in the faces of whole crucified peoples. God is manifested in hiddenness, namely, in locations of poverty, death and suffering. According to Gustavo Gutierrez, for example, theology must be nourished by the manifestation of God in the weakness and scandal of the cross. 'But, again like Job, we cannot keep quiet: we must humbly allow the cry of Jesus on the cross to echo through history and nourish our theological efforts.'[2] Central to many of the liberation theologians is the intimation that in order to speak most persuasively of the living and liberating God, the reality of death-dealing evil must be confronted. In the face of evil, God seems to be absent from, or indifferent to, suffering in history and nature. Thus, the reality of affliction makes reflection on the hiddenness or absence of God a necessity in our contemporary context.

2. Idolatrous forms of theodicy

Far from generating an apathetic philosophy or a complacent fascination with evil, sensitivity to hiddenness of God on the part of both Simone Weil and the liberation thinkers gives birth to a creative attention to where God is most truly revealed: in cross, negativity, conflict, suffering. Unlike certain forms of theism, Simone Weil insists that the struggle with the hiddenness of God resists the temptation to find a theoretical explanation to the problem of evil or rationally to justify God's existence. In succumbing to this temptation, modern forms of theism too often evade the reality of affliction in spite of, or perhaps because of, the creation of modern, argumentative solutions to the problem of evil or 'theodicy'.[3] Philosophical atheism and agnosticism certainly are no more thoughtful on the question of evil than modern theism. God's existence is often denied or ignored on explicitly rational grounds. Missing from their accounts is a creative reflection which seeks to confront and inspire resistance against the crescendo of evil in our time.

Along these lines, Simone Weil argues that modern forms of theodicy are often idolatrous subterfuges which distract and avert our gaze from human affliction. The destruction of such idols makes a struggle with evil in history and nature on the one hand, and even with God on the other, a necessary moment of theological and philosophical thought. Thus for Simone Weil the struggle with the hiddenness of God is anything but apathy and indifference towards either the afflicted or God, as in much of atheism and agnosticism. Indeed, she insists that only those who know God's presence can cogently speak of God's absence. Struggle with God's hiddenness is the path to contact with God. 'For it seemed to me certain, and I still think so today, that one can never wrestle enough with God if one does so out of pure regard for the truth. Christ likes us to prefer truth to him because, before being Christ, he is truth. If one turns aside from him to go toward the truth, one will not go far before falling into his arms.'[4] In her reading of Greek tragedy, she will claim that wisdom is born only of suffering, pain, struggle; grace comes violently.

Struggle with God and the concrete experience of human suffering are necessary encounters for shedding light on the conflict between God and human suffering. Reflection on the question of evil cannot be isolated from the existential confrontation with suffering, Weil claims. The question of evil resists theoretical solutions and brings the intellect to its knees. Thus, for Simone Weil, glimpses of the meaning of suffering will only be detectable through the concrete encounter with suffering. 'I feel an ever increasing sense of devastation, both in my intellect and in the centre of my heart, at my inability to think with truth at the same time about the affliction of men, the perfection of God, and the link between the two. I have the inner certainty that this truth, if it is ever granted to me, will only be revealed when I myself am physically in affliction . . .'[5] In such a vision, wisdom is born of suffering.[6]

3. Contact with the afflicted

In the mystical thought of Weil, moreover, spiritual exercises have the task of, first, emptying the mind and spirit of any idols and, second, of cultivating the attention. In reference to the issue of suffering and evil, no less, spiritual practices train one's attention to make possible a reception of the vision of God (theoria) in the face of affliction. Simone Weil insists that rational speculation alone is futile in shedding light on the question of evil. The separation of theory and practice only exacerbates the thoughtlessness on the question of evil fostered by modern forms of theodicy. Attention to the hiddenness of God in Simone Weil, therefore, proceeds by spiritual exercises (of an intellectual, aesthetic and ethical nature) and the painful struggle to endure and transform suffering itself. In Simone Weil, contact with the afflicted (living and dead) is the most significant avenue for contact with God. It is here that God's seeming absence manifests a hidden presence. It is in the faces of the afflicted that we discover that the void of God is a greater plenitude than the presence of all worldly entities.[7] Contact with God is given to us through the hiddenness of God. 'Contact with human creatures is given to us through the sense of presence. Contact with God is given to us through the sense of absence. Compared with this absence, presence becomes more absent than absence.'[8]

II. The ambiguity of 'God'

1. The prophets

The classic Hebrew prophets surely understood and were fascinated by the struggle with divine absence or hiddenness. In the book of Deuteronomy, for instance, Yahweh tells Moses (the archetypal prophet): 'I shall hide my face from them. I shall see what their end will be' (Deut. 31.17,18; 32.20). With this sense of God's hiddenness, Jeremiah complains of his plight in life, of his undeserved suffering. 'Why did I come forth from the womb, to see sorrow and pain, to end my days in shame?' (Jer. 20.18). In the figure of the 'suffering servant', Isaiah expresses the cries and woes of one who is innocent, one who is despised and rejected by all, a man of suffering (Isa. 53). His suffering is *not* seen as punishment for sin and disobedience. Elsewhere Isaiah laments what appears to be God's absence. 'Where is he who brought them up from the sea with the shepherd of his flock? . . . Oh that you would rend the heavens, that you would come down . . .' (Isa. 63.11–64.2). Isaiah then concludes that God has hidden his face from us (64:6). Such a prophetic struggle with divine hiddenness is inextricably linked with an awareness of the presence of power, violence and oppression in history and society. In this light, the prophets express an acute awareness of, or we might say fascination with, God's hiddenness.

2. Martin Luther: theology of the cross

In relation to the question of divine hiddenness, B. A. Gerrish claims that in the thought of Luther there is an uneasy tension between the hidden knowledge of God manifested in the historical, incarnate and crucified Word of Jesus Christ on the one hand, and a hidden knowledge of God outside of Jesus Christ on the other. He has helpfully referred to these as Hiddenness 1 and 2, respectively.[9] Hiddenness 1 articulates a classic theology of the cross championed in a creative way by Luther. In this tradition, God is disclosed in hiddenness: in the folly and scandal of cross and death. The glory of Christ is not recognizable in visibly dramatic nor beautiful ways. Far from being the object of adoration, Christ is the object of scorn, revulsion and disgust. Christ's glory is hidden beneath affliction.

Hiddenness 2 is more disturbing and problematic. In his most troubled moments, Luther suggests that even after the historical manifestation of God in Christ, there is much that remains unknown about God. The 'concealed and dreadful will of God . . .', Luther says, remains 'the most awesome secret of the divine majesty'.[10] Why is the hidden will of God dreadful for Luther? One aspect of that answer concerns the question of predestination. The dreadful will of God is none other than the decision of God to consign a portion of humanity to perdition. While the incarnate God does not desire the death of the sinner, the *Deus Absconditus* damns a majority of the human race. Luther: 'He does not will the death of the sinner – in his Word, that is. But he does will it by that inscrutable will.'[11] Is there a struggle within God himself between contradictory elements of mercy and wrath, or Hiddenness 1 and 2, respectively? Does the death of Christ on the cross reveal a God struggling on behalf of humanity against the wrath of an unknown God?

While for Luther the experience of the ambiguity of God and of the ostensible conflict within God is related to the issue of predestination (which he relates to the tragic notion of fate!), for Simone Weil and many liberation theologians the conflict is most apparent in the issue of evil and affliction. The seeming chaotic rule of force and violence in history and nature is the source for her reflections on the hiddenness of God. Why God allows affliction and force to destroy human life is the troubling source of her thoughts on the apparent conflict within God. 'The great enigma of human life is not suffering but affliction . . . It is not surprising that disease is the cause of long sufferings, which paralyse life and make it into an image of death, since nature is at the mercy of the blind play of mechanical necessities. But it *is* surprising that God should have given affliction the power to seize the very souls of the innocent and to possess them as sovereign master.'[12] It is not surprising, then, that Weil notes the fact that the scriptures speak of a God who both manifests and hides himself. She quotes Isaiah 45.15 in the Latin, '"*Vere tu es Deus Absconditus*" . . . The universe both manifests and hides God.'[13]

David Tracy sums up the importance of the issue of Hiddenness 2 very well: 'At the very least, this literally awe-ful and ambivalent sense of God's hiddenness is so overwhelming, so powerful, that God is sometimes experienced as purely frightening, not tender: sometimes as an impersonal reality of sheer power and energy signified by such metaphors as abyss, chasm, chaos, even horror, sometimes as a violent personal reality . . . It is Luther (here quite different from even Augustine and Pascal) who will speak of what the ancient Greek tragedians named "fate" in ways Aeschylus and Sophocles, if not Euripides, would have understood.'[14] In this manner, the question of Hiddenness 2 is an interpretation of and confrontation with the absence or violence of God. In the face of destructive evil, the question of theodicy irrepressibly comes to the forefront.

3. The Greeks: not ignoring the dark

Simone Weil claims that an awareness of the presence of misery and suffering in human life is the genius of the 'bitterness' of the Greeks, especially of the tragedians. Such a bitterness cannot be equated with a despairing fatalism or sadness, she insists. In reference to Greek poetry she maintains that 'no matter how painful they are, these dramas never leave us with an impression of sadness'.[15] Indeed, she will insist that it is with the moderns that a despairing sadness dominates the interpretation of tragedy. In short, Greek tragedy is not nihilistic in Weil's reading. Indeed, for Weil, the genius of Greek tragedy is the beauty of the poetry. In an honest and artistic fashion it illuminates the truth of the human condition in a way which refuses to ignore the dark and brutal forces in history and nature.

The greatness of the Greeks, then, should be seen in light of their genius to illuminate the destructive presence of force in human life, as in war, and yet to despise it. Weil contends that their tragic vision is a lucid construal of the terror of history, of the harsh realities of suffering and violence. Greek tragedy, and Homer in particular, shows how force turns all subject to it into a 'thing'. In Simone's essay on the *Iliad*, she cogently makes evident that force destroys all roots of memory as well as the inclination to rebel. 'Curses, feelings of rebellion, comparisons, reflections on the future and the past, are obliterated from the mind of the captive; and memory itself barely lingers on.'[16] As in the 'Dark Night' of John of the Cross, memory is lost and emptied when confronted with affliction.

III. Theodicy: theory or practice?

In her lifetime, Weil directed her attention against many instances of destructive force, i.e., colonialism, in the modern world.

1. The modern situation

She was tireless in reproaching the French government and people for their cruelty and indifference to the people of Algeria.[17] Weil harshly reproached Europeans for their oppression and exploitation of African people. On the issue of the colonization of the Americas, she showed a contempt for those who sought to justify or mitigate the offence in any way. Prior to the beginning of World War Two, Simone Weil even dared to suggest that a world war, while certainly not desirable, might prove to be punishment for the cruelty of modern European nations toward colonized peoples. 'When I think of a possible war, I must admit that the dismay and horror such a prospect evokes in me is mingled with a rather comforting thought. It is that a European war can serve as the signal for the great revenge of the colonial peoples, which will punish our unconcern, our indifference, and our cruelty.'[18]

The issues of colonization and war in the modern world were, indeed, one major reason why Weil repudiated the idea of progress so harshly. Any honest attention to the presence of violence and suffering in modernity belied, for Weil, any optimistic faith in reason and progress. 'For those dreamers who considered that force, thanks to progress, would soon be a thing of the past, the *Iliad* could appear as an historical document; for others, whose powers of recognition are more acute and who perceive force, today as yesterday, at the very centre of human history, the *Iliad* is the purest and the loveliest of mirrors.'[19] There is a dark underside to the ostensible progress of the modern Western world. The histories (or rather non-histories) of whole groups of oppressed and subjugated peoples challenge modernity's confident celebration in enlightenment and evolution. The presence of force and affliction is still a harsh reality in the modern world.

2. The cross of Christ

'Thus do the gods justify the life of man: they themselves live it – the only satisfactory theodicy!';[20] Simone Weil would agree with this saying of Nietzsche; indeed, the only satisfactory theodicy is through a divine solidarity with the affliction of the world. 'The Cross of Christ is the only source of light that is bright enough to illumine affliction.'[21] This does not suggest that the mystery of evil has a theoretical solution, even in the form of the cross of Christ. The cross of Christ is, rather, a divine response to evil and the model for our response to the presence of affliction. It is a response which is marked by a solidarity without a reason for suffering. It remains silent.

The possibility of a reconciliation between Hiddenness 1 and 2 in Weil suggests that the cross of Christ is not merely a redemption of sin, but includes as its central meaning the embrace of affliction and the transformation of radical evil. Thus, in Weil's view, the passion of Christ cannot be reduced to a consequence of the Fall. 'Thus it is true to say that the Incarnation and the Passion are and are not consequences of Adam's disobedience.'[22] Human misery, she claims in this context, is misunderstood if reduced simply to a matter of sin. The suffering of God on the cross is more than a response to a moralizing reading of the Fall. Instead, it is a response to the question of evil by God living it.

The vision of Weil ends hopefully. She insists that a Christian reflection on affliction is not a 'morbid preoccupation with suffering and grief'.[23] The cross of Christ is the path to an insight and awareness of the presence of evil in history and nature. When this awareness is joined with a loving attention to the affliction of others (*agape*), participation in the cross becomes the location of God's reconciliation with humanity and with God's very self. In order for this to be possible, the mystery of evil must be posed as insoluble and rational explanations eschewed. The example of God disclosed in Christ is the inspiration for a response to evil which loves and is just without a why.

> The benefactor of Christ, when he meets an afflicted man, does not feel any distance between himself and the other. He projects all his own being into him. It follows that the impulse to give him food is as instinctive and immediate as it is for oneself to eat when one is hungry. And it is forgotten almost at once, just as one forgets yesterday's meals. Such a man would not think of saying that he takes care of the afflicted for the Lord's sake; it would seem as absurd to him as it would be to say that he eats for the Lord's sake. One eats because one can't help it . . . The supernatural process of charity . . . does not need to be completely conscious. Those whom Christ thanks reply: 'Lord when . . .?' They did not know whom they were feeding.[24]

3. Transform the affliction

The gift of justice and love dispenses with a 'why'. Just as there is no 'why' to evil, there is no 'why' to compassion for the afflicted. To seek explanations for the mystery of evil in this manner is harmful to charity. 'And to try to find compensations, justifications for evil is as harmful for the cause of charity as it is to try to expound the content of the mysteries on the plane of the human intelligence.'[25]

The refusal to seek solutions to the problem of evil is, therefore, the basis for compassionate and just action in Simone Weil. Action is inspired by the silencing of explanatory 'whys'. When the question 'why' arises, our thought must turn in the direction of a practical concern to alleviate or, if possible, transform the affliction of others. 'Why has it been allowed that he should go hungry? While one's thought is occupied by this question, one proceeds automatically to find bread for him.'[26] The loving and just praxis without a why is related, for Weil, to Christian *agape*. In the faces of unknown and strange Others, love makes its presence felt.

Notes

1. 'Why, O Lord, do you stand far off? Why do you hide yourself in times of trouble? In arrogance the wicked persecute the poor – let them be caught in the schemes they have devised . . . Rise up, O Lord; O God, lift up your hand: do not forget the oppressed' (Psalms 10.1–2,12). With the prophets the hiddenness of God often expresses God's anger at the sins of the people – Isaiah pleads with God to forget his anger and to return to God's people. 'There is no one who calls on your name, or attempts to take hold of you: for you have hidden your face from us, and have delivered us into the hand of our iniquity' (Isa. 64.7).

2. See Gustavo Gutierrez, *On Job*, Maryknoll 1987, 103.

3. Along these lines I am indebted to David Tracy's unpublished essay 'Evil, Suffering, Hope: The Search for New Forms of Contemporary Theodicy'.

4. See *Waiting For God*, New York 1951, 69.

5. See *Simone Weil: Seventy Letters*, London 1965, 178.

6. Weil often mentions Aeschylus in this regard. See Aeschylus, *The Oresteia: Agamemnon*, 176–83, trans. Richmond Lattimore, Chicago, 1953, 40. Weil also mentions Hesiod for the expression of a 'wisdom born of suffering'. See *Works and Days*, 195–223, trans. Dorothea Wender, Harmondsworth 1973, 65.

7. Lucien Goldmann, in *The Hidden God: A Study of Tragic Vision in the Pensées of Pascal and the Tragedies of Racine*, London 1964, claims that the tension between God's absence and presence is central to a tragic vision. He especially thinks such is the case in Pascal. 'But we must add that for Pascal, and for tragic man in general, this hidden God is present in a more real and more important way than any empirical and perceptible being, and that His is the only essential presence that exists. That God should be always absent and always present is the real centre of the tragic vision' (37).

8. See *The Notebooks of Simone Weil* (2 vols), London 1956, 239–40.

9. See B. A. Gerrish, *The Old Protestantism and the New: Essays on the Reformation Heritage*, Chicago 1982, 134.

10. Ibid., 136. See Martin Luther, *Bondage of the Will*, trans. John Dillenberger, in *Martin Luther: Selections from His Writings*, New York 1962.

11. Ibid., 137.

12. See *On Science. Necessity, and the Love of God*, London 1968.

13. See *The Notebooks of Simone Weil* (n. 8), 149.

14. See David Tracy, 'The Tenderness and Violence of God: The Return of the Hidden God in Contemporary Theology', *Lumière et Vie*, Spring 1996. Luther indeed understood the tragic vision of fate. In *The Bondage of the Will* Luther explicitly discusses fate in the poets (he mentions Virgil in particular). In his words: 'Those wise men knew, what experience of life proves, that no man's purposes ever go forward as planned, but events overtake all men contrary to their expectation.'

15. See *Intimations of Christianity Among the Ancient Greeks*, London 1987, 19.

16. 'The *Iliad* or the Poem of Force', in *Simone Weil: An Anthology*, ed. Sian Miles, London and New York 1986, 169.

17. See Simone Petrement, *Simone Weil: A Life*, 319, 325.

18. Ibid., 297.

19. 'The *Iliad*' (n. 16), 63.

20. See *The Birth of Tragedy*, New York 1967, 43.

21. See *On Science, Necessity, and the Love of God* (n. 12), 194.

22. See *The Notebooks of Simone Weil* (n. 8), 236.
23. See *On Science, Necessity, and the Love of God* (n. 12), 192.
24. Ibid., 190–2.
25. See *The Notebooks of Simone Weil* (n. 8), 341.
26. See *The First and Last Notebooks*, London 1970, 94.

III · Conclusions

Overcoming Evil

Hans-Eckehard Bahr

A final, all-embracing overcoming of evil – that would be the messianic state of absolute redemption. Certainly, however, time and again in history there are interruptions of evil. In the twentieth century in particular, more than in any other era, it has been possible to contain and indeed transcend evil politically, through political communication (peace treaties). We shall discuss this limitation of political evil by civil communication first.

I. Non-violent resolutions of conflicts (macro-structural factors)

In the twentieth century, great social movements have for the first time been able to have their demands for justice and peace met no longer through revolutionary violence but with resolutely non-violent forms of intervention in 'evil' political structures. One may recall:

– *Gandhi's* significance for the ending of British colonial rule in India, his social therapy for ending conflicts in Third World zones;
– *Martin Luther King's* role in introducing a multi-ethnic social situation in the USA; his non-violence as a ritualization of political conflicts within a democratic framework;
– the ending of the *Vietnam war* as a result of very heterogeneous but primarily non-violent peace movements in the USA after 1963.

One may recall the capacity of silent majorities in the population to learn as something new in education for peace, but also:

– the strategy of isolating *the Latin American military dictatorships* before the world public morally, and consequently economically, by pacifist protest actions, e.g. by compelling a general amnesty for all political prisoners, by fasting in church buildings, and by hunger strikes in public places in Bolivia (January 1978: Domitila) and Argentina (from 1977, the mothers of the Plaza de Mayo).

One may also recall

– the pedagogy of non-violence in the social *literacy experiments* in Sicily (Danilo Dolci), in California (Cesar Chavez) and in northern Brazil (Helder Camara);
– the role of the *Irish peace movement* in the minimizing of violent regional conflict;
– the bloodless removal of the military dictatorships in *Greece, Portugal* and the *Philippines*;
– the rediscovery of imaginative and non-militant forms of communication in the Western European *ecology and peace movement* since 1981.

But what was absolutely new in the twentieth century was the overcoming of political 'evil' in the state dictatorships of *East European Communism* by the civil resistance of citizens, i.e. from within and not from the outside, say by NATO. That was successful in Prague, Warsaw and Leipzig. There the opponents did not allow themselves to be drawn into lynching the hostile opposition, the soldiers and the Party officials; only in Bucharest was there such excessive vengeance. On the contrary, the civil protesters prevented a blood bath by beginning from the anxieties of their political opponents, and indicated to these Communist Party opponents that they had a chance of survival (priestly action versus a mentality of vengeance).

Today it can be said that without the example of Martin Luther King, the Leipzig Monday prayers of 1989 and the protest demonstrations attached to them would not have taken so decisive a civil course. And in *South Africa* too, resolute lessons have been learned from the experiences of the US Civil Rights movements. Anyone who wants to study the conditions for an interruption of political evil must therefore primarily tackle Martin Luther King's theology and pedagogy of conflict.

II. Individual conditions for non-violence (subjective factors)

1. Empirically safeguarded

Another striking new element is the discovery or rediscovery of non-violent forms of resolving conflict in intersubjective communication. From the early discoveries of classical psychoanalysis (Freud) to the almost infinitely differentiated practices of therapy in the present, this discovery has been safeguarded by experiential science and is not simply the moral postulate of an ethics of conviction. In principle, conflicts can be integrated. Here, however, it is presupposed that one 1. has confidence in one's own capacity to change and in the capacity of one's partner to relearn, and 2. knows the rules of the game for a peaceful resolution of conflict.

Psychological research into aggression has recently developed some approaches which could be utilized for a 'constructive' way of dealing with 'evil'. Those concepts from the humane sciences are theologically significant which primarily aim at a constructive transformation of destructive behaviour. Such a predominantly 'therapeutic' interest is needed to supplement the hitherto predominantly diagnostic, analytic and ethical interest in theology.

In view of the many scientifically based theories about the origin of aggression and the lack of strategies of communication aimed at non-violence, it is urgently necessary for us to direct all our energies to such therapeutic strategies. For a long time, so many experiences of the integration of conflict have been available that we can set a positive scale of successful communication over against the current negative scale of research into aggression. Just as we can understand aggression as innate in human beings, as acquired during life and as conditioned by frustration, so we can also understand a readiness for peace as a potential of human nature, acquired during life and conditioned by competence. Here special significance would need to be attached to the concept of competence (Erich Fromm). Thus those psychological capabilities would need to be discovered which can change all those conditions in the environment which particularly frequently entail aggression and violence.

2. Freud and Gandhi combined

Peace research with a theological orientation thus sees itself confronted with the task of combining with other disciplines in an inter-disciplinary collaboration the two experiential levels of non-violent action mentioned above: I, the political, external and international level; and II, the inter-personal internal level. Thus I find it extremely attractive to compare and to synthesize the constructive results of peace research orientated on sociology with those of crisis therapy orientated on individual psychology.

Such peace studies have only recently been initiated. The American psychoanalyst Erik H. Erikson represents the newly-aroused interest of the human sciences in the USA. He points out how Gandhi and Freud, each with his method of truth, have contributed towards helping us to grasp the two greatest dangers for human freedom. The first is the way in which human beings are so enslaved by anxiety about the radically other that they think that they have to annihilate or suppress this other. The second is that they are correspondingly so enslaved by the sense of threat from their own nature that they attempt overwhelmingly to suppress it. All this, he emphasizes, is common to all human beings, and human beings are threatened equally by their inner and outer compulsions to dominate.[1] These compulsions are as old as the social evolution of human beings and in our time need to be controlled by insight. This insight is still new and hardly proven; it is untrained and uncertain in its application. But the task of universities is to build a bridge between the oldest and the newest in human beings.

3. *Violence can be overcome*

For many historians and anthropologists, as for educationalists and theologians, so far a violent 'resolution' of conflicts (interpersonal, social and international) has been the painful but unchangeable reality of human history. This view is based on the basic moral and political assumptions of the struggle for life (*homo homini lupus*) as the only principle of reality which is empirically adequate, or on the premise of social philosophy that destructiveness is given by nature and has an irreversible ontic content. The theology of original sin also belongs here as a system which legitimates power politics. In these circumstances and under the spell of the most recent history of suffering endured by many peoples, the perspective of peace all too easily rigidifies into a Manichean gaze. To many people the political life of societies still seems to be a closed structure of power and violence, and here a loss of dialectical power, a dangerous loss of hope, is evident. The surprising emergence of non-violent forces, the breakthrough of the counter-forces of a new political humanity, the limitation of evil, all this is then concentrated in hopeless exceptions which only seem to confirm the terrible rule of 'always the same violence'.

Thus today, unintentionally, we have a new mystification of violence: its omnipresence makes people blind to the quite other history and presence of non-violent popular and civil rights movements. But today the need to recall the latter is greater than ever. At all events, in the tradition of these movements we find those counter-experiences to which the implementatiom of a peace policy can relate in the wider international sphere and any conflict therapy can relate in the smaller interpersonal sphere, since these counter-experiences are for the first time empirically verifiable. For the first time in the history of scholarly study there is a stimulus to investigate the subjective and social conditions of non-violent behaviour in conflicts, not from a merely moral impulse stimulated by an ethic of conviction, but from the empirically demonstrable fact that we can practise a repertoire of behaviour to diminish crisis.

III. The anthropology and therapy of political evil

1. Inner co-operation: Martin Luther King

In Spring 1966 I experienced the black Nobel Peace Prize-winner Martin Luther King for the first time. In Chicago I was able to take part in a dramatic attempt to transcend the racist structures of public life, a communal configuration of social evil. On 3 September 1966 there was a march by black and white civil rights supporters through the hostile 'white' suburb of Cicero. I recall a prototypical scene: a nineteen-year-old man threw a sharp stone at Martin Luther King which knocked him over. Hardly had King got up again than he asked to speak to the man, now, immediately: 'The stone that he threw is a telephone conversation with me,' King told us, 'a contact that didn't get through.'

The black civil-rights worker was physically attacked twenty-two times: stones, stabbings, shots. And each time he made an attempt to speak with his attackers, to come into contact with the threatening strangers, to find inner co-operation in the outward confrontation. He sought contact in the qualitative sense of an open, genuine communication which was not just strategic, in the crazy hope that even someone with a dangerous mania could still change. This talking is the age-old attempt to take the other seriously as a person. 'In this search,' I heard King add, 'one also rediscovers one's own humanity.'

2. Four dimensions in overcoming violence

How does one build up an inner co-operation in an outward confrontation? How does one reach the stranger, the depths of the other? How does one 'dissolve' evil? Are not all these programmes mere dreams? I can see four dimensions in such communication by contact, as a transformation of evil.

i. Fear

First, in myself, as in any stranger who confronts me, I begin from the same fear of being stripped, of losing face, of showing weakness. Therefore – thus the usual reflex – I must arm myself with strength, and make myself as strong both inwardly and outwardly. The equilibrum of armaments, the security pacts of the 1980s, were the analogy to this in foreign politics.

ii. An interest in reconciliation

Now if I begin from the same anxieties, can I not also begin from the same interest in reconciliation? Can I not also begin from the generosity which draws us forward, and achieve something better? That would be quite a different, a second, dimension of contact. The difference here is like that between day and night, whether I define the other in terms of his or her anxiety or whether, in another dimension, I also claim his or her, and my, creative possibilities of communication. So I strive to preserve myself by trusting the stranger, and perhaps *vice versa*. In that case I succeed in getting close to the threatening stranger only if I present myself to others as someone who I not yet am. That would be a programme which was orientated on the capacity of the other to change.

iii. Equality of the living

Here something fundamentally new enters the confrontation, with a terrifying strangeness which takes us beyond the dryness of mere external parity. I mean that resolute hold on a humanity which is common to all human beings, an equality of the living which also embraces the stranger. As often as I succeed in basing myself on this and making contact with it, I can even venture to open myself in such a way that the other gets the greatest possible scope for a sovereign attitude which is more free from anxiety.

iv Contact with human beings

A third dimension of contact with strangers comes into view here. Maria Hippius, Countess Dürckheim of Rütte, fleeing through Mecklenburg, found herself in open country with a troop of Russian soldiers. There were howls and cries of anxiety. Then she tells how suddenly she made eye-contact with a sixteen- or seventeen-year-old Russian. Minutes later the soldiers let her go, after the young Russian had spoken to the others. Looking at, being looked at: understanding can come about like that in a flash. It is an understanding beyond words, which we know from everyday life in far less dramatic situations, in the office, while travelling, buying something, particularly in incidental communications. Something succeeds there which does not succeed in larger matters. At any rate, here in a flash the destructive drive is transformed into living energy, eroticism. Thanatos to Eros, even in the supermarket. But in the long run such mystical contact comes about only in the moment in which I attach, or am attached, myself, to the deepest energies of creation, to the strongest communicative forces in the world: you are a human being, and I am a human being. That would be the fourth dimension, a last one which one cannot bring about by social technology.

A process is needed which – to put it in mythical language – 'breaks the spell' when people depart from a provocation to violence, from self-destruction or anxiety about freedom, and are brought over to the side of their better possibilities. Human beings are in fact always 'possessed' by tendencies towards anxiety or violence, i.e. by 'evil', to use the symbolic language of the Bible. As long as we are under the spell of such evil, all the ethical admonitions in the world are no use. In that case we need a reminder of the opposite forces in us that goes much deeper. That such an ethic of conviction brings tangible success in practice is something that I have learned in my research into the genesis of the new youth violence in Germany.

3. Transformation to creative personal achievements? (Youth violence in Germany 1997)

Here is an example of an experiment in positive youth work from the eastern part of Berlin. A young woman pastor had been able to persuade young people to collect medicine for White Russia. Now there were disturbances in the same part of the city caused by extreme right-wing youths. Their slogan was that one must help the Russians in their own countries so that they do not come to us. The young woman took up this slogan and suggested to the aggressive young people that they should take the medicines to Minsk, and risk an adventure convoy. That was the key word. It gave them a kick; they set off, and were welcomed in Minsk. On their return they were appreciated positively for the first time in their Berlin suburb as well. The Munich psychotherapist Thea Bauriedl comments on this. 'When someone has done something good, then he is in much less danger of becoming violent. He becomes violent when he feels excluded.'

This example from Berlin contains some presuppositions for that interruption of violence which has long been called for by representatives of established public authorities:

1. The youths were taken out of their milieu of unemployment and self-rejection. At least once, the victims became active.
2. Far beyond the programme which occupied them, they participated inwardly in a social action which was felt to be a good one.
3. This action provided the opportunity for all of those who took part in it to discover their own capabilities, whether technical, logistical or communicative. In one small place they could do something of their own, something that had nothing to do with money and individual possession, but with other people.
4. That generates pleasure in life. Here it becomes clear that whereas appeals remain external, the experience of competence and pleasure in life leads to the solidarity which is so much called for. In this way an

experience of meaning arises – of course, as elsewhere, in partial spheres and in a fragmentary way.

5. Another feature of the example from East Berlin seems to me to point to the future: here a desire for experiences and a wish for adventure are taken seriously as forms of discovering oneself and the world, as a way of crossing boundaries and taking risks.

6. Finally, here one encounters the growing concern not just to occupy young people therapeutically from above and outside, but to stimulate them by activating pleasure in life, independence and group co-operation.

Could not this self-mobilization in something small and creative be the presupposition for overcoming evil? Cannot the spell of its fascination for young people be broken in this way?

Translated by John Bowden

Notes

1. See Erik H. Erikson, *Life History and the Historical Moment*, New York 1975, 188.

Theodicy: Dissonance in Theory and Praxis

David R. Blumenthal

Between acceptance and protest

Theodicy is grounded in cognitive dissonance. Reason and common sense tell us that a loving God does not kill innocent children, or exterminate loyal followers, or punish the righteous. And yet, such things do happen in the world created and governed by the good God. Theodicy is the art of resolving that dissonance.

Introduction: Resolving the dissonance

The logical options are not many. One option is to repudiate all, or part, of God. Thus, one can deny that there is a God at all, removing God completely from the issue. Or, one can reject God's full power, asserting that God has no way of stopping evil, for since human beings have the freedom to choose evil or good, evil must be the work of human beings and not God. Or, one can disavow God's total goodness, claiming that God can indeed do evil on God's own initiative. Another option is to repudiate evil, asserting that whatever happens is really good. Thus, one can affirm that evil is a punishment for sin. Or, one can assert that it is a warning against greater sin. Or, one can claim that evil is a test of virtue, a purification. Or, one can maintain that it is a stumbling block whose overcoming is a merit and protection against other personal or national evil. Yet another option is to argue that, since God is qualitatively other, one cannot know why God does what God does, nor can one really hold God accountable for God's acts. Therefore, one should have faith, or trust, in God's goodness and leave ultimate moral judgments to God's inscrutable wisdom. In the image of scripture, 'God hides God's Face', to which the proper response is faith and loyalty. The history of theodicy is the history of the presentation and rehearsal of such arguments, with appropriate supporting texts, and not much is new under the theodical sun.

A new start might be made by asking, 'What makes any theodical argument a "good" argument?' Put more precisely, 'What resolution to cognitive dissonance is a "good" resolution?' A good resolution, it seems to me, should meet three criteria as fully as possible. First, it should leave one with one's sense of reality intact. It should affirm what one knows to be the facts, no matter how unpleasant they may be. Second, it should leave one empowered within the intellectual-moral system in which one lives. It should allow one to live the basic truths by which one orders one's life, no matter how counter-intuitive these truths may seem. And, third, it should be as intellectually coherent as possible. In the matter of theodicy, this means that a good argument does not deny reality as it can be – evil; nor does it deny the basic structure of the religious world – a good God; and, it does not leave one unduly torn by contradiction and incoherence.

I. A problem in theodical theory and praxis

1. God: not always good

The best theodical argument, to my mind, is to limit God's goodness; that is, to assert that God is usually, but not always, good. I argue that the evidence from the reality of the Holocaust does not allow common sense or reason to assert that evil is somehow good. One cannot, in good conscience, say that the Holocaust is somehow a punishment, or a warning, or a test, or a hidden merit against a worse evil. I also argue that the continuing felt spiritual presence of God in the lives of believers and in the collective life of the Jewish people does not allow reason or common sense to deny God's existence. God is an accepted part of who religious humanity is. I further maintain that common sense and reason do not allow one to deny or limit God's power. Rather, the very assertion of God's ongoing presence in creation implies that God is at all times active in nature and in human history. Finally, I contend that God's ongoing presence and power implies God's ongoing, direct and indirect, moral co-responsibility in human affairs. The following image conveys the sense of God's ongoing responsibility in human affairs, even for the evil that humanity does. If I give the keys to the car to my son and he injures someone, who is responsible? Surely, he is factually, morally and legally responsible. Yet, even if I have done all in my power to educate him properly in the skills and responsibilities of driving, I too, in some way, am very much responsible if my son has an accident. I have an encompassing moral co-responsibility for what happens in his life. So, too, God and humanity. God has an encompassing moral co-responsibility for what happens in his life. So, too, God and humanity. God has an encompassing moral co-responsibility in the action of humans by virtue of being Creator.[1]

Considering these four arguments, together with others, and drawing on the Zoharic tradition of Jewish mysticism as well as on an intact sense of the reality of the Holocaust, I am willing to say that God, from time to time, acts in evil ways; that God, at unpredictable moments in the ongoing divine-human relationship, does evil. Moreover I argue, together with the sources, that this propensity for evil is inherent in God, that any such evil act is not always a function of prior human sin. I set forth all this carefully in my book *Facing the Abusing God. A Theology of Protest*,[2] where, drawing on data from the field of child abuse, I named this dimension of God 'abuse' and proposed 'worship of God through protest' as a legitimate response.'[3]

2. Four arguments

'Ethical, spiritual, and theological nihilism,' she said.[4] '*Reductio ad absurdum*, unsustainable theology,' he said.[5] Others have joined the chorus, even as all have commanded my courage and expressed high praise for other aspects of the book. Why? What is the force behind such vehement rejection of what seems to be a rather reasonable, and even traditional, solution to the theodical problem? The first criterion for resolution of cognitive dissonance has been met: one's sense of reality has been left intact. The Holocaust remains unadulterated evil in every sense of the word.

The second criterion for resolution of dissonance – empowerment within one's general intellectual and moral-world view – has also been met. Worship of God through protest, in thought and in prayer, is an empowering response to the theodical problem. Theological and liturgical protest, precisely as a form of worship and ongoing relatedness to God, fulfills the second criterion of a good resolution to cognitive dissonance. This response of protest also has the virtue of being a long and hallowed tradition with roots in the Bible (the Book of Job; Book of Lamentations, especially the first two chapters; the 'lament psalms', especially Psalm 44; and so on) as well as in the rabbinic tradition.[6]

The resistance to the resolution of our post-Holocaust and abuse-sensitive theodical situation which I have proposed stems from the third criterion: contradiction. But of what? I have contradicted the idea of God's *omni*benevolence; I have shattered the idea that God is *always* good. The weighty philosophical-theological apparatus of the tradition presupposes that God is omnibenevolent, that God always acts with justice and, hence, that any evil in creation cannot emanate from God. The logic of God's perfection precludes God's imperfection. Since God is perfect, God is always good; therefore, God cannot be, or contain, evil in Godself or even in God's actions. Indeed, most of the philosophic-theological part of the tradition denies any human form or feeling to God (with the occasional exception of intellect and/or love)[7] and, so, would certainly deny evil to God. When I argue, then, that God does encompass evil, even though I can call to arms many passages from Scripture[8] as well as Zoharic and Lurianic theology, I have broken a 'logical' taboo. In asserting evil as a component of God Godself, I have crossed a line in theodical theory.

3. Healing: A seriatim process

In the area of theodical praxis, too, I have crossed a line. Work with survivors of the Holocaust and of child abuse shows that, for all survivors, healing is not a one-way process; healing is simply not linear. One does not work at healing and, then, 'get over it', 'get released', 'forgive and go beyond it', or 'convert [sic] away from it'. The opposite is true: one rages, one deals with one's rage by mourning the past and empowering oneself, but the past returns. Survivors who lose a parent or a child, or who become patients in a hospital, or who read about and identify with the abuse of others, or who are subject to the infirmities of aging – all have recurrences of the helplessness of the abusive time in their own lives. They all re-experience the powerlessness of their earlier trauma. With that powerlessness comes the rage, again and again, and it must be dealt with, each time, by mourning, empowerment and protest.

I argue, therefore, that healing itself is a *seriatim* process, a tacking into the wind, an alternation between empowerment and desire for revenge, between acceptance and protest, between love and rage.[10] How could it be otherwise? The past cannot be erased or ignored (at least not for any length of time). It must be coped with by mourning and empowerment, and by protest. Further, this must be done, not simultaneously, not linearly, but in an alternating rhythm. This healing-by-tacking is not unethical; it is not disintegrative; it is not a miring down in a cyclic process. Rather, it is a moving forward by alternating directions. It is sewing with a backstitch, repeatedly. It is integrative – more integrative than healing procedures that urge survivors to 'forgive and go beyond', to 'be healed once and for all'.

To put it differently: a sculpture must be seen from all sides and this cannot be done simultaneously but *seriatim*; one must walk around a sculpture to see it fully. Like sailing, viewing a sculpture is a better image of what life is, and ought to be. Healing and protest alternate in sculpting one's life, not once but repeatedly – which makes this approach good art and, therefore, compatible with good theology. Or again: alcoholics never say they are 'cured', they always refer to themselves as 'recovering alcoholics'. Similarly, survivors are not 'healed'; they are 'recovering survivors'. (We all might do well to follow the modesty and realism of alcoholics and survivors and refer to ourselves as 'recovering sinners'.)[11]

4. Worshipping God through protest

(a) A liturgy of rage and protest

Theodically, the same analysis holds. To respond to the dissonance of the theodical situation by demanding that one 'get over' one's anger at God, or that one 'forgive and go beyond' one's rage against God, is to undermine the healing process. It implies a 'linear' image of healing in the theodical situation that does not seem to me to be realistic or even morally proper. Demanding that a survivor of child abuse or the Holocaust 'get beyond' his or her theodical anger impugns the moral sense of the survivor and casts doubt on the ethical integrity of the divine-human relationship.[12] Protest, when one thinks God is wrong, is a better option, psychodynamically and theologically. It preserves the God of the texts and traditions, as well as the moral sense of humanity, God and the tradition. Asserting God's presence in human history and then worshipping God through protest is a better path for those for whom God's ultimate sovereignty and responsibility are real, though it does require a willingness to face God without flinching.

The images of tacking into the wind in order to advance, or backstitching, or walking around a sculpture, or recovering from addiction are better paradigms: one prays the liturgy of rage and protest vigorously and honestly. Then one tacks to a liturgy of joy and blessing. One turns yet again to a theology of courageous challenge. And then one tacks again to a theology of belonging and empowerment.[13]

Within Jewish tradition, the value-concept[14] of covenant requires the Jew to affirm God's action in history and to protest it when necessary, even as one alternates protest with community-building. Covenant grounds one's right to protest and indeed makes protest obligatory. Covenant also obliges active and concrete commitment to community. However, each is obligatory in its own due time. In setting forth this interactive and realistic understanding of healing, especially in the theodical situation, I have crossed a line in the praxis of theodicy.

(b) Fierce resistance

In sum: theodical theory, especially in its philosophic-theological form, requires a perfect God who cannot be, or contain, evil and who cannot act in clearly evil ways. Only the affirmation of the omnibenevolence of God is admissible. Theodical praxis, especially in its philosophic-theological mode, requires the final setting-aside of all rage against God and the willing and complete submission to God's good will. The cognitive dissonance of the theodical situation is thus dealt with, especially in the philosophic-theological tradition, by denying the evil of the event and by affirming the absolute goodness of God.

By contrast, theodical theory, as I envision it, requires one to limit God's omnibenevolence and hence to assert that God is capable of evil. Further, it demands that one recognize that challenge and protest are theologically legitimate options. Theodical praxis, as I see it, requires, not pious rationalized acceptance of dissonance, but a serious fight against dissonance through protest as a form of thought and worship, used always in alternation with a theology and praxis of empowerment, joy and blessing.

In spite of its roots in scripture, in the mystical theological tradition, and in reason and common sense, the proposal I have made has encountered fierce resistance. Reading my book is difficult, emotionaly more than intellectually. Criticism has been vehement beyond the usual scholarly rigour. There have even been those who have argued that a theodicy that inculpates God cannot, by definition, be called a theodicy; that is, that a theodicy that does not justify God is not a theodicy.[15] I, too, was emotionally and physically ill before I wrote the concluding section and I remain tense and ambivalent when I use the liturgy I myself proposed. The disproportionate character of this reaction suggests that more than a 'logical' taboo has been broken, theoretically and practically, in this theodicy. The stormy response suggests a storm. What, then, is at stake in a theodicy that names God an abuser and suggests a therapy that progresses *seriatim*?

II. Roots of resistance or, why God must always be good

1. God's goodness: A pre-judgment

The fierce resistance to a theodicy rooted in God's abusiveness stems from the set of commonsensical questions: Who wants a God who is abusive?! Who wants to know that the Ground of all reality is evil?! If God is truly abusive, who wants to have a relationship with such a God?! If the Ground of all reality is really evil, who wants to worship such a Being?! Diane has put it very well:[16]

If God is an abuser, the adult non-sick response should be to turn away permanently from him. Why stick around and be hurt more? . . . I do not trust omnipotent God not to abuse his power. I do not trust omnipotent God to care for me. I much prefer omnipotent God to stay away than to be involved intimately in my life.

So has W. Farley:[17]

. . . ultimate power or reality [as you describe it] is not ineffable, 'my thoughts are not your thoughts'. This power is not mysterious at all; it is perfectly clear what sort of power this is. It is the power of the sadist and the traitor. The nightmare of the abused child is not a bad dream, nor even an aberration caused by a sick or wicked parent; it is the proper and true expression of divine power and reality . . . and more important, religiously, I can't imagine worshipping an abusive father. Psychologically, it is neurotic and ethically it is immoral.

These questions are not unreasonable, yet they are not strictly rational questions. They are rooted in the idea that God must be omnibenevolent. More accurately, they are grounded in the assumption that God must be good and cannot be evil, in the prior commitment to the total goodness of God. The fierce objection to the theodicy of abuse and *seriatim* healing flows from a very, very deep pre-judgment about the non-evil, omnibenevolent nature of the divine, the evidence from the common-sense view of reality as well as from the tradition to the contrary notwithstanding. What is the source of this pre-judgment? Why is it so strongly held?

Making use of Freud's operational terms without necessarily subscribing to his mythological structures[18] can be helpful here. Briefly, 'transference' is the psychological process in which one projects one's experience of one's parent on to a third person and then reacts to that person as if she or he were one's parent. When such a process takes place with a non-personal subject such as one's place of work, the state, or God, it is usually called 'projection'. People are very, very deeply attached to the qualities they 'transfer' to others and to the values they 'project' on to institutions and ideas.

As noted, the commonsensical questions mentioned above express a prior commitment to, and a pre-judgment of, God's total goodness. Of course humans *want* God to be totally good and humans do *not want* God to be abusive. Humanity needs some comfort in the face of the pain one experiences when one confronts a universe that is at best indifferent and often cruel. Humans need to know that, in the end, one will be justified. What could be more human? So human beings project this total goodness on to God and put up with the cognitive dissonance that results when one juxtaposes reality and God.[19] Freud, in a famous essay, foresaw this.[20]

Invoking Freud is surely not enough to establish an hypothesis as true. Nonetheless, acknowledging the truth of projection as a human psychological process and admitting, further, that the total goodness of God is a projection are important steps toward psychological and theological truth. 'Truth has legs'; yet, 'the seal of the Holy One, blessed be He, is truth'.[21] The fierce resistance to a theodicy which admits evil in God, then, stems, first, from the strength of the projection of omnibenevolence onto God.

An equally fierce resistance has been observed with respect to the proposal of *seriatim* therapy as noted above. Again, the question arises, why? What motivates a resistance that goes beyond the usual critical reflection that any new proposal generates? Again, an answer is to be found in the projection of omnibenevolence. The same impulse that moves human beings to want to know that ultimate reality is good also moves one to want to know that hostility, enmity and rage are not the permanent lot of human existence. Hate consumes. Jealousy devours. Revenge burns harshly. Better to wipe the slate clean, to repress, indeed to purify oneself of such powerful negative emotions.

The evidence shows and common sense experience confirms, however, that trauma is not so easily swept aside, pain is not so easily relieved, and the rage that trauma and pain produce is not so easily purified from one's being. It is, therefore, unrealistic to expect these powerful aspects of human experience to be permanently set aside. Yet, in spite of the unrealistic dimension of the task, human beings design systems of psychological and religious therapy that aim to accomplish exactly what cannot be accomplished. If one aims at the unrealistic goal of 'going beyond' anger and rage, then that is a goal set more by desire than by reasoned analysis and reasonable expectation. It is a desire for, and projection of, *human omnibenevolence* – quite contrary to what we know of human nature and behaviour. Such projection is understandable, as is the projection of omnibenevolence on to God, but it is, nonetheless, projection. The second reason for the fierce resistance to the theodicy of abuse and *seriatim* therapy, then, stems from the strength of the projection of ultimate goodness on to humanity.

2. A problem of Christians

Christians have a third reason for fiercely objecting to the theodicy I have proposed.[22] Feminist scholars have been among the most outspoken in pointing out that God's insistence on crucifying his son is the essence of an abusive relationship.[23] Still, mainstream Christian reading of the

Gospel story centres on Jesus' loving acceptance of God's decree. While this response is also very rabbinic,[24] most Christian understanding turns suffering into the chief means to salvation. Crucifixion-and-redemption becomes the central pillar of Christian doctrine and praxis. This, in turn and quite naturally, affects the attitude toward therapy among therapists who are also serious Christians, as well as among Christian clergy. For such helping persons, the proper resolution of rage and anger is submission and acceptance; that is, 'getting beyond' rage, 'converting away' from anger. Indeed, for therapists and clergy brought up in Western (i.e., Christian) culture, the goal of healing is to be salvific; that is, to be a one-time, one-way healing process.

A theodicy that admits that God can indeed do evil and that centres upon continuing confrontation and protest as part of a *seriatim* religious healing process is a theodicy that questions whether God was right in insisting on crucifying his son. More important, it raises the issue of whether the son should not have protested rather than have submitted and accepted that abusive act. (Jesus does question in Gethsemane but resolves it into acceptance.) Most importantly, a theodicy of abuse and protest suggests that Jesus' followers through the ages – Christians – should be rebelling against the theology of crucifixion-and-redemption and should be following instead a salvific path of challenge and protest integrated into a praxis of *seriatim* healing. A theology of divine evil and human objection thus questions some of the basic theological and salvational roots of Christianity, as well as the extension of those roots into psychotherapeutic attitudes and goals.

III. Conclusion: mature God/mature servant

I, too, wish that there were a peaceful, totally healing solution to the theodical problem. I, too, yearn for the wholeness and reconciliation that should come from the resolution of the emotional and cognitive dissonance. Part of the fascination with evil is, indeed, the lure of the harmonious resolution of the dissonance between theology and reality embodied in the theodical problem. But it is not so and cannot, in my view, be so. Further, the attempt to make it so is itself the natural, but wrong, expression of the very deep human wish and yearning for full spiritual peace. The alternative, while it is less sanguine, is however more realistic and hence, in my mind, better.

Most persons reach the point of realizing that their parents are (or, were) not perfect; perhaps that they are (or, were) not even really good, really loving. Some touch this realization and shy away from it as quickly as

possible. Most come to it and go on to consider in what ways their parents
are (or, were) *also* good. That is, most people eventually come to a more
balanced view and appreciation of the full range of qualities in their
parents. This is called 'maturity', 'growing up'. One need not throw out
the parent with the bathwater. One need only be as clear and as fair as one
can, and then arrange one's patterns of relatedness.

The same is true of our relationship with God. Human beings do not
need to have a perfect God. Rather, humans need to have a realistic view
and appreciation of God. Humanity needs to see all sides of God. Then,
and only then, can human beings, as individuals and as groups and
cultures, arrange their patterns of relatedness to God. In a theodicy of
abuse and protest, one need not throw out God with the purifying waters.
Nor need one hide one's head in the sand and deny God or some aspect of
God's ever-present being. Rather, one can accept the good and the evil,
praising where fitting and protesting where appropriate. One can alternate between love and challenge, between acceptance and protest. Just as
having a mature understanding of one's parents enables one to become a
more mature person, so having a mature understanding of God enables
one to become a more mature servant. A theodicy of abuse and protest set
in the context of *seriatim* healing, although it challenges the more usual
views, seems to me to accomplish this and hence would appear to be a
'better' theodicy, in theory as well as in praxis.[25]

Notes

1. This analogy raises an interesting question about the difference between direct
and indirect responsibility. Did I 'cause' the accident? Or, did I 'allow' it? I did
neither factually and, hence, bear no legal responsibility on either count. However, in
a deeper moral sense, one can, nonetheless, affirm my encompassing moral co-responsibility. In that context, the question of direct or indirect causation as the ground for
moral responsibility is not relevant. So, too, in theology: God has an encompassing
moral co-responsibility for creation. Whether God 'causes' or 'allows' evil is not
relevant. The question is: 'Is God co-responsible? Can God be held morally accountable, together with us?' To this I, grounded in the tradition, propose an affirmative
answer.

2. Here the concept of encompassing moral responsibility and the distinction
between factual-legal and moral-theological responsibility are not sufficiently developed, though both of these ideas are very much within Jewish tradition.

3. *Facing the Abusing God. A Theology of Protest*, especially chapters 15–16. The
use of the term 'abuse' is new in Jewish sources. The argument is not new, as I
demonstrated there clearly. For a recent defence of personalist God language, see
D. Blumenthal, 'Three is Not Enough? Jewish Reflections on Trinitarian Thinking',
available on my website (see biographical note).

4. W. Farley in *Facing*, 213–24.

5. N. Solomon, review of *Facing, Journal of Jewish Studies* 48.1, Spring 1997, 195–7.

6. All of this is carefully laid out in *Facing*, chapters 17–18.

7. This is the disagreement between those philosophical theologians who advocate the *via negativa* and those who advocate 'essential attributes'. See *Facing*, 6–31, 246–8; 'Croyance et attributs essentiels dans la théologie juive médiévale et moderne', *Revue des études juives*, 1994, 152:415–23; and 'Three is Not Enough' (above n. 3).

8. See *Facing*, 240–6; 'Who is Battering Whom?', *Conservative Judaism* 45.3, Spring 1993, 72–89; and 'Confronting the Character of God: Text and Praxis', in *God in the Fray: Divine Ambivalence in the Hebrew Bible*, ed. T. Beal and T. Linafelt, forthcoming (both also available on my website).

9. The last phrase is taken from J. Rike, review of *Facing, Journal of the American Academy of Religion* 65.1, Spring 1997, 206–9, though I have heard the criticism she voices widely.

10. See *Facing*, chapter 5, for the basic image and follow the Index for its application to religious healing.

11. The analogy to sculptures and to alcoholics resulted from dialogue after publication and is not included in *Facing*.

12. Denying God's existence or providence, or limiting God's power, is also rooted in a rectilinear image of healing.

13. The liturgy of protest also includes a request, indeed a demand that, in consonance with the laws for a repentant offender, God must ask forgiveness of the Jewish people for God's part in the Holocaust (*Facing*, 263–4 for the theology and 286–99 for the liturgical formulations. On 297, n. 21, where I even suggested a possible liturgical formulation in this mode to be inserted into the 'Lord's Prayer', the text should read: 'Our Father . . . Forgive us our sins, as we forgive those who sin against us. Ask forgiveness of us, as we ask forgiveness of those whom we have wronged . . .').

14. On this term, see M. Kadushin, *The Rabbinic Mind*, New York 1952, reprinted several times.

15. This is the ultimate argument of the friends of Job.

16. *Facing*, 198–9, italics original.

17. *Facing*, 217, 221, italics original.

18. See B. Wolstein, *Theory of Psychoanalytic Therapy*, New York 1967, discussed in *Facing*, 12, 188.

19. What is interesting is that W. Farley admits that I project evil in formulating my idea of God, but is not clear that she (and others) project goodness in her (their) formulation of the idea of God (*Facing*, 217).

20. S. Freud, *The Future of an Illusion* (available in many editions).

21. Aleph-Bet of Rabbi Akiva, second version, *Batei Midrashot*, ed. A. J. Wertheimer, 2, 404, and Talmud, Shabbat 55a; Maimonides, *Mishne Torah*, 'Hilkhot Teshuva', 14,3; cited in *Facing*, 237.

22. On my indebtedness to the Christian theological enterprise, see 'From *Wissenschaft* to Theology: A Mid-Life Recalling', available on my website (see above).

23. See, for example, J. C. Brown and C. R. Bohn (ed.), *Christianity, Patriarchy, and Abuse*, Cleveland, OH, 1989.

24. See, for example, Talmud, Ta'anit 8a and the martyrology in the Yom Kippur penitential service. For an anthology of some of these texts, see C. G. Montefiore and H. Loewe, *A Rabbinic Anthology*, New York 1974, chapter 28. This, however, did not become the main rabbinic response to suffering.

25. To be sure, there are those who would argue the contrary: the fascination with evil results from a desire to undermine the legitimacy of the good God. Not resolving the theodical problem but holding on to it is itself a desire to keep the problem alive and, hence, to avoid total submission to the omnibenevolent God. I hear the argument but am not persuaded. Contending with God requires very deep faith and, in the final analysis, is rooted in a (mature) loving relationship. See the articles cited above, to which add 'My Faith is Deeper Now', *Jewish Spectator*, Spring 1995, 40–3; also available on my website.

Saving from Evil: Salvation and Evil Today

David Tracy

I. Introduction: the problem

The most basic anthropological principle of Christianity is this: one may have as radical an understanding of evil and sin as necessary as long as one's understanding of grace and salvation are equally radical. The contemporary question of the fascination of evil be illuminated by that principle as follows: anyone can possess as radical a fascination with evil as he may need (or thinks she needs) as long as the *fascinans* and *tremendum* power of the Good is equally radical. To test this thesis in contemporary Christian life demands three basic considerations: first, a general phenomenology of salvation from evil; second, the need to incorporate total liberation as part of any phenomenology of salvation; three, the need for theologians to face not just the fascination with evil so prominent among contemporary cultural élites but to consult and learn from the real experts in evil: the suffering, poor and oppressed as they have left their reflection in their narratives, songs, actions and rituals. To move beyond fascination is to move towards suffering peoples everywhere.

II. Christian Salvation: Its Basic Elements

1. *Releasement from evil*

The Christian understanding of salvation begins with an experiential claim. That claim is this: a Christian experiences a state of some releasement from some experienced evil, and in that very release, a sense that this healing is from God. However fragmentary such experiences may be – even for those whom William James named the 'intense religious cases', the saints and mystics – these experiences are sensed by Christians as both real and salvific. The experience is inevitably dialectical. The experience is, first, an experience of release from some powerful bondage: a release from guilt by the forgiveness of sin, a release from the bondage of an anxious sense of radical transcience, from anxiety in the face of death, from anxiety in the face of the seeming absurdity of existence, from the bondage of a sense of being trapped without hope of release in systemically distorted structures of one's individual psyche or of society and history or even from bondage to the contemporary fascination with evil.

The experience is, at the same time, an experience of fascination: a releasement *to* some new way of existing as an authentic human being; an experience of freedom for living in the world without ultimate mistrust of existence; a freedom for accepting the created world and one's own finitude as essentially good; a freedom for accepting the fact of one's own acceptance by God despite sin and guilt; a freedom for facing death as not the final world; a freedom for acting in solidarity with others in the trust that such actions ultimately do make a difference; a freedom for accepting experiences of peace, joy, and understanding as manifestations, however fragmentary, of the presence of God.

2. *Gift from God*

All such experience, like *all* experiences, bear interpretative elements including the interpretative element of fascination. Aside from the complexities of hermeneutic theory, this simply means that: (*a*) there is no experience without some understanding; and (*b*) every act of understanding is itself an act of interpretation.

In the Christian case, the interpretative elements in these experiences of fascination, releasement and wholeness are many. For such experiences are named not only 'releasement' but 'salvation'. This means that a Christian experiences and interprets these salvific experiences as both gift and task from God. More precisely, these experiences are Christian experiences of *faith in* the God who in Jesus Christ disclosed what ultimate reality is (viz., the holy, fascinating and terrifying mystery of embracing and encompassing love). These experiences disclose as well to the Christian who we are and who we can become (viz., finite but estranged human beings who can be released from bondage by grace and thereby be freed to follow Christ's way of radical love of God and neighbour).

3. *Through Jesus Christ*

The experience of releasement-wholeness as an experience of Christian salvation is, therefore, Christianity construed as an experience of response to the God disclosed in Jesus Christ. That is, in Christian terms, an experience of faith. Faith implies but does not fundamentally *mean* faith as a *belief that* certain cognitive meanings are true. Rather Christian faith, as an experience of salvation, fundamentally means a *belief in*, a trust in, acceptance of, even fascination for God. From that interpretative experience of releasement and wholeness as an experience of radical trust in and loyalty to God all else flows: the recognition that this experience is gift, grace and calling; the recognition that the saving initiative in the experience is God's; the recognition that this saving initiative comes to us through Jesus Christ. From the acknowledgment of our salvific experience of releasement, grace and wholeness we also learn much else: the acknowledgment that this experience of releasement from whatever compulsive bondage once trapped us is also a releasement to a new way of life, a way modelled on the way disclosed in the ministry, teaching, death and resurrection of Jesus the Christ, i.e., the one who did and, in present individual communal Christian experience, does decisively manifest the nature of the ultimate reality with which we all must deal as the God who is love.

4. *Continuous interpretation*

The fundamental Christian witness to salvation is a witness which is grounded in those primary interpretative experiences of 'salvation' as releasement from bondage and releasement to this new way of Jesus Christ. In this salvific experiential context, therefore, the fundamental Christian confession remains 'I (we) believe *in* Jesus Christ *with* the apostles'. This confession does not read, note, 'I believe in the historical Jesus', nor 'I believe in Christ', nor, 'I believe *in* the apostles'.

The confession means what it says: 'I (we) believe *in* Jesus Christ *with* the apostles.' To observe the force of the preposition 'in' is to note the grounding of Christian salvific experience (both individually and communally) in the reality of God's disclosure in Jesus Christ. To add the phrase 'with the apostles' is to recall the need for further theological criteria for interpreting what we mean by 'the apostles'. This is also to recall how, in a historically and hermeneutically conscious age, we late twentieth-century Christians can interpret ourselves as in continuity with those first witnesses to Christ.

On this reading, therefore, any modern Christian attempt to understand salvation and evil must attempt ever new formulations of what the basic phenomenon of 'Christian salvation' is. These new formulations will prove, at best, relatively adequate interpretations of all the most fundamental questions in our present quests for release and for a new way of authentic freedom and justice.

In fact this process of continuous interpretation of Christian salvation has occurred, is occurring, and, as long as Christians continue to experience salvation at all, will continue to occur. Why otherwise the strange contemporary silence (at least in progressive Christian theological circles) on such classic Christian metaphors for redemption-salvation as 'ransom from the devil', 'expiating sacrifice', and theories of 'satisfaction' and 'satispassio'. Why otherwise the need to find better ways (as with Rahner, Balthasar, Geffré, Tillich, Küng, Ogden, Cone, Ruether, Sobrino, Gutierrez, Gebara, Metz, Jossua, Schillebeeckx, Jeanrond, Schüssler, Fiorenza, et al.) to discern which fundamental questions (mortality, transcience, forgiveness of guilt and sin, fascination with evil, anxiety over meaninglessness, the many bondages of oppression) are the central ones today: crucial for any particular interpretation of what Christians are saved from and what way of life they find themselves released *to*? Why otherwise would suffering, that contrast-experience *par excellence* (Schillebeeckx), provide such diverse clues to provoke different Christian 'searches for salvation' (or even, with Rahner, a search for an 'absolute saviour') while at the very same time suffering can become a central moment in the kind of personal transformation central to the Christian interpretation of the way of Christ (Moltmann) as the way of self-sacrificial love for God and neighbour even unto death.

Through all these many interpretative salvific experiences by and through all theological interpretations of those experiences, however, there does seem to exist a unity. That unity lies in the basic elements outlined above: in sum, Christian 'salvation' is an experience of releasement from bondage and releasement to a new, fascinating as well as terrifying, authentically free way of life; 'salvation' is that experience experienced and interpreted as gift and task disclosed by Jesus Christ as the decisive manifestation of the God who is pure, unfounded Love (Ogden); 'salvation' is the experience-acceptance of a releasement from the bondage of guilt-sin, the bondage of radical transitoriness and death, the bondage of radical anxiety in all its forms including the contemporary fascination with evil. 'Salvation' is also releasement *to* the engifted task to have faith in that God and all those whom God loves – i.e., all creatures (not only human creatures) – by following the Christian way.

As the political, liberation and feminist theologians have taught us all, renewed interest has arisen in one further question of salvation today; granted this general phenomenology of the Christian understanding of salvation, should we also say that Christian 'salvation' is the empowering gift and command for Christians to enter wholeheartedly into the struggle for political, cultural, and social liberation? Is salvation properly construed as a total liberation which demands political action? This lies at the heart of much contemporary Christian debate on and fascination with the issues of salvation and evil today.

III. The fascination with salvation and liberation

In one sense it is obvious that Christian salvation can be described through the metaphor 'liberation'. In both the Jewish and the Christian understandings of salvation, liberation by God from bondage has been a central biblical and post-biblical metaphor: classically in Exodus and in the prophetic trajectories. Moreover, 'bondage', the correlate to liberation, is frequently used to describe what we are saved or liberated *from*. Indeed, 'bondage' is a constant basic element through all the shifts of metaphors for the more positive salvific experience (salvation *for* or *to*) in the history of Christian reflection. More exactly, death, suffering and guilt-sin are frequently described in terms of 'bondage' which only divine liberation-salvation can liberate or save us from. In the classical Christian perspective, there is (or should be) little controversy on the appropriateness of describing salvation as total liberation; from guilt-sin, from death and transience and, in principle, from any bondage which entraps us.

1. Systemic distortion

The force of the metaphor 'bondage' may be clarified, in modern terms, by comparing it with an analogous secular term: 'systemic distortion'. 'Error' has always been a problem for any reflective consciousness. Since the Greek Socratic enlightenment through early Western modernity, the belief has endured (as Nietzsche described it, the *optimistic* belief of Western reason) that 'error' was real, even pervasive, but at the same time error was removable through the use of reflective reason – in discussion, dialogue and argument. If our only problem is one of cognitive 'error', then bondage to evil is an inappropriate metaphor to describe our state, just as liberation is an overloaded metaphor to describe our release from that state.

But what if something other than error is at stake? Then we need a term deeper (and more fascinating?) than 'error' to describe our situation. We need as well some resources other than the more familiar Western discussions of conscious reason to 'heal' that situation. Perhaps this great modern narrowness on 'rationality' (not ancient 'reason') accounts for the contemporary fascination with evil as a phenomenon very real today, a phenomenon beyond error. In contemporary secular terms this latter state may be described as 'systemic distortion'. The term does not mean conscious error but unconscious though systemically functioning distortions. The now classical strategies of Freud, Marx, Nietzsche and feminist criticism are, one and all, exercises in spotting not errors but systemic distortions (ideologies in the 'hard' sense). The argument is characteristically that such distortions (sexism, racism, classism, elitism, homophobia, rationalism, Eurocentrism, antisemitism) can be shown to exist through such critical accounts of modern 'reason' as Freud's, Marx's, Nietzsche's or feminist criticism. The post-modern argument also insists that we need new strategies (e.g. 'critical' theories as distinct from 'traditional' theories) to account for and sometimes remove or at least alleviate these unconscious but systemically operative distortions that both plague and fascinate us.

All these typically 'post-modern' hermeneutics of suspicions (not mere critique) are, of course, fundamentally exercises in the same trajectory of Western reason. Yet that reason has now been chastened from its former 'optimism' on evil. It has been reformulated to provide partial strategies of 'critical theory' to spot the illusions in our radically pluralistic and radically ambiguous accounts of 'reason' and evil. But these strategies, however anti-Enlightenment in their interpretations of reason-error, are also continuations of the history of freedom through the use of reason. More than most 'modern' or 'liberal' accounts of our dilemma, however, these post-modern accounts of systemic distortions (or illusions) lend themselves to the metaphorical language of 'bondage' and to an anti-Enlightenment fascination with evil (so well witnessed as early as Goya's fascinating and frightening paintings in 'The Sleep of Reason').

Even in its best exercises of reason and freedom, the purely 'autonomous ego' of liberal modernity did not usually understand itself as a shattered self either very aware of radical evil or very cognizant of the possibility of radical self-delusion. Indeed, even for Kant, radical evil was the primary reality which forced his late reflections on 'religion' even after he completed his three great critiques. That the classical Christian interpretations of salvation and post-modern secular readings of our situation are fascinated both with evil and with the existence of systemic distortions (illusions) and not mere errors should be instructive to us all. Indeed, the illusion pervading fascination is our real problem. Clearly, the Buddhist and Hindu accounts of our 'primal ignorance', in their distinctive ways, share this same kind of general belief that 'primal ignorance' is not a mere cognitive error which clear thinking and sharper agreement could remove.

2. Emancipation – redemption

Where Christian construals differ from post-modern secular accounts is also clear: Christian understandings of 'evil' and 'sin' can (and should) include a recognition of such systemic distortions as sexism, racism, classism, antisemitism, etc. and yet the Christian understanding of 'sin' is not exhausted by these accounts – above all, since sin is theocentrically interpreted as sin against God. Just as importantly, Christian understandings of salvation can (and again should) include an insistence on the need for joining wholeheartedly in the post-modern journeys of political, cultural, social emancipation and freedom. Yet again, Christian salvation, as grounded in God as origin and goal of all human actions, cannot be achieved through the sole use of some new emancipatory method or struggle, but at the same time must be committed to and involved in that struggle.

Metz is surely correct to insist that 'emancipation' and 'redemption' (in his terms) are not synonymous but must be dialectically related in any Christian understanding of redemption/salvation. The liberation theologians and the feminist theologians are also surely correct to insist that the often forgotten, perhaps even repressed, biblical metaphor of 'liberation' is an excellent category to articulate why Christians understand 'freedom from' and 'freedom for' as the crucial categories for understanding any Christian salvation.

There is also no need to deny the primordial Christian character of 'freedom from' guilt-sin. Nor, in my judgment, is there any need to deny, on inner Christian grounds, the hope for 'freedom from' death in Christian salvation – as the powerful memories in the songs and narratives of suffering of all oppressed peoples show so clearly. At the same time, there is no need to retreat into an individualism or a weak personalism in understanding Christian salvation. Indeed there is every good reason for Christian theologians aware of the pervasive reality of social and political structures in all our exercises of freedom and the actuality of unconscious psychic and linguistic structures in all our exercises of fascination to abandon all purely individualist and personalist accounts of salvation in order to face squarely the contemporary fascination with evil and the contemporary demand for salvation as liberation. But where shall we best turn today to reflect on both evil and salvation? To some extent, of course, the artists as 'the antennae of our race' are excellent guides to the contemporary fascination with evil. To an even larger extent, however, we need to turn to all those peoples who have suffered throughout our history and in the massive global suffering of today. They are our truest artists and articulators of the forms of evil, suffering, fascination and hope.

IV. Where to turn to learn how to move beyond mere 'fascination' with evil?

Facing evil and suffering

Modern thought, both philosophical and theological, has been relatively impoverished on the issues of suffering and evil. Most modern theodicies have ended in failure. Surely the history informing those theodicies took a turn for the worse from the Enlightenment puzzlements over the Lisbon earthquake to the collapse of modern theodicies and humanistic anthropodicies in the interruptive and *tremendum* impact of the Holocaust on all Western senses of modern progress. The attention of many has been turned away from modern self-confidence to face the evils and sufferings of whole peoples – the colonization (not 'discovery') of the Americas, Africa, parts of Asia and Oceania; the horrors of black slaves in the Middle Passage; the famines of Ireland and Russia; the Armenian massacres; the Gulag Archipelago; Cambodia; the Aids plague; Bosnia; Rwanda; Burundi; Sudan; etc. On and on the list runs with relentless severity. Voltaire's *Candide* yields to Dostoyevsky's *The Brothers Karamazov*. Ivan's protest atheism (I am tempted to say his real atheism, to distinguish it from the paper-thin, unserious theories that often bear that honourable name) still challenges Alyosha's vision of a compassionate, suffering Christ empowering Christian solidarity with all suffering and Christian resistance to all evil. Indeed, since Nietzsche, Alyosha Karamazov has become, for many, the very symbol of the honest Christian: facing evil beyond fascination; without any final explanation for evil and suffering, indeed resisting evil and aiding the suffering but finally silent in the face of the mystery of evil and God, and turning anew to study the mission, message and fate of Jesus as the Christ in order to see again the compassion of God.

All thought must be interrupted by the great counter experiences of suffering, especially the suffering caused by the horrifying historical evils whose echoes no serious thinker can avoid. To develop a *logos* on *theos* – a theology – today is to start by facing evil and suffering. To develop a theology today is to reject modern theodicies in their modern forms of purely theoretical solutions which, however finely tuned in argument and however analytically precise in concept, are somewhat beside the point – the point of facing with hope the horror while still speaking and acting at all by naming and thinking the God of genuine hope.

2. Ethics of the other

In the contemporary fascination with evil, as in so many important theological issues, the religious sensibilities of religious peoples –

especially oppressed and marginalized peoples in their songs, their endurance and protest, their struggles for justice, their forms of prayer and lament, their liturgy, their laughter, their reading of the scriptures – are often wiser, not only religiously but also theologically, than the carefully crafted theodicies of the professional theologians. Eugene Genovese has shown this with clarity in his fine study of how the ante-bellum slaves of the United States read the accounts of suffering, struggle and liberation in Exodus far more accurately than the official preachers and theologians of the period did. African-American theologians, with their recovery of the slave narratives, the folk tales, the trickster figures, the spirituals and blues, continue this religious-theological heritage. Several post-Holocaust Jewish theologians – Arthur Cohen, Emil Fackenheim, Irving Greenberg – have also developed new forms for theological thought – like Fackenheim's reading of Elie Wiesel's work as 'mad midrash', like Greenberg's radicalized new covenant theology and Cohen's amazing rethinking of Rosenzweig.

Surely a large part of the reason for Levinas' impact on Jewish and Christian thought today is his recovery of an ethics of the other as first philosophy. It is Levinas' philosophical ability, after the Holocaust, to develop an ethic of the other based on the core insight that the face of the other says 'Do not kill me!' The recovery of formerly repressed and marginalized voices of women in all cultures over the centuries from the scriptural period forward is, of course, the clearest and strongest voice of all across all the new forms and contents invented by feminist, womanist and *mujerista* theologies.

All these new forms for theologies are grounded in a refusal to turn away from evil, to refuse its mere fascination and sometimes charm, to refuse to embrace any theodicy – indeed any theology – that ignores the evil and suffering endured by so many peoples. Recall the haunting refrains of suffering and resistance, of strength, hope and surprising joy (not mere fascination) in the songs and tales of oppressed peoples everywhere. Surely theologians can hear again the strength and tragedy in the songs and comic tales of the famine Irish and their descendants in the Troubles. We can recall the tragic joyous plaintive undertones of so much Latin American music and its brilliant literature of magic realism. Surely we can sense the refusal to avert our eyes (more accurately our souls) from the nightmare that has been the history for so many Slavic peoples. Indeed, every oppressed people has such tales to tell, such new forms to invent – and these narratives of enduring suffering and resisting evil with strength and often even joy are the narratives most needed to empower and transform whatever form a theological response to the contemporary fascination with evil may take in our post-modern day.

3. Western culture: ambiguous

Modern Western culture, I am convinced, will one day be read as deeply ambiguous – at once liberating and narrowing for the spirit and the mind. Unlike any other culture of which we have knowledge, unlike Western culture itself in the pre-modern period, and unlike much of Western culture today in that elusive set of movements in search of a name and thereby calling itself with the non-name post-modernity, modern Western culture believed that we not only could but should separate thought from feeling, content from form, theory from practice. Despite the many great accomplishments of modernity (accomplishments which, considering the alternatives of societal and ecclesial obfuscation, mystification, intolerance and even tyranny clearly still demand defence, including theological defence), modernity has also proved impoverishing in its inability to face evil and suffering with something better than occasional outbursts of fascination. This must include not only personal suffering but especially the suffering which modernity's own historical success has often caused: the evils endured by whole peoples, cultures and groups both outside and within modern Western culture. It is those peoples who will ultimately teach us all to face evil, suffering and liberation with something far stronger and sounder than the fascination of evil which pervades so much of our contemporary Western culture, both popular and elite.

Bibliography

1. Pablo Richard et al., *The Idols of Death and the God of Life: A Theodicy*, Maryknoll 1983.

2. Christian Duquoc and Casiano Floristan, *Where is God? A Cry of Human Distress*, Concilium, 1992/4.

3. Elizabeth A. Johnson, *She Who Is: The Mystery of God in Feminist Theological Discourse*, New York 1992.

4. Edward Schilebeeckx, *Christ: The Experience of Jesus as Lord*, New York and London 1980.

5. Schubert M. Ogden, *The Point of Christology*, San Francisco and London 1985.

6. Eugene Genovese, *Roll, Jordan, Roll: The World the Slaves Made*, New York 1976.

7. I have expanded on the reflections of the final section of this article in D. Tracy, 'Evil, Suffering, Hope', in *The Proceedings of the Catholic Theological Society of America* (1995). The entire proceedings include the reflections of many and diverse theologians on these issues and merit careful study.

Contributors

HEDWIG MEYER-WILMES was born in 1953. She studied Catholic theology, pedagogics and German in Münster and then worked as a teacher of religion and a parish assistant before lecturing in theology at the Catholic University in Nijmegen. She is a visiting professor in women's studies and theology at the Catholic University of Leuven and is also President of the European Society for Women's Theological Research. She has written *Rebellion on the Borders*, Kampen 1995, and edited *Over hoeren, taarten en vrouwen die vorbijgaan*, Kampen 1992 (with Lieve Troch), and *Zwischen lila und lavendel*, Regensburg 1996.

Address: Erasmusplein 1, NL 6525 NT, Nijmegen, The Netherlands.

GREGORY BAUM was born in Berlin in 1923; since 1940 he has lived in Canada. He studied at McMaster University in Hamilton, Ontario; Ohio State University; the University of Fribourg, Switzerland; and the new School for Social Research in New York. He is Professor Emeritus at the Religious Studies, Faculty of McGill University, Montreal. He is editor of *The Ecumenist*. His recent books are *Essays in Critical Theology* (1994), *Karl Polanyi on Ethics and Economics* (1996), and *The Church for Others: Protestant Theology in Communist East Germany* (1996).

Address: McGill University, 3520 University Street, Montreal, PQ, H3A 2A7, Canada.

HERMANN HÄRING was born in 1937 and studied theology in Munich and Tübingen; between 1969 and 1980 he worked at the Institute of Ecumenical Research in Tübingen; since 1980 he has been Professor of Dogmatic Theology at the Catholic University of Nijmegen. His books include *Kirche und Kerygma. Das Kirchenbild in der Bultmannschule*, 1972; *Die Macht des Bösen. Das Erbe Augustins*, 1979; *Zum Problem des Bosen in der Theologie*, 1985; he was a co-editor of the *Wörterbuch des*

Christentums, 1988, and has written articles on ecclesiology and christology, notably in the *Tijdschrift voor Theologie*.

Address: Katholieke Universiteit, Faculteit der Godgeleerdheid, Erasmusgebouw, Erasmusplein 1, 6525 HT Nijmegen, Netherlands.

PAULO SUESS was born in Cologne in 1938. He studied in the universities of Munich, Louvain and Münster, where he gained his doctorate in theology. He has lived in Brazil since 1966; since 1988 he has been head of postgraduate studies in mission in São Paulo and since 1996 Vice-President of the International Association for Mission Studies. His most important books are *Volkskatholizismus in Brasilien*, Mainz 1978; *A conquista espiritual da América Espanhola, 200 documentos – século XVI*, Petropolis 1992; *Evangelizar a partir dos projetos históricos dos outros*, São Paulo 1995.

Address: Caixa Postal 46–023: CEP 04046–970 São Paulo, Brazil.

ROSEMARY MUIR WRIGHT is a Senior Lecturer in the School of Art History at the University of St Andrews, Scotland. She has written on the iconography of mediaeval manuscripts and is currently working on the imagery of the Virgin Mary in the Renaissance period and the strategies of the artists to preserve that sacred distance despite the new technical discoveries of pictorial space. She is author of *Art and Antichrist in the Middle Ages*, Manchester 1995, and has written articles for *Word and Image*, the *Journal of Mediaeval History, Cosmos*, and in various conference proceedings.

Address: School of Art History, University of St Andrews, Fife, Scotland KY16 9AD, Scotland.

CATHERINE KELLER is Professor of Constructive Theology in The Theological and Graduate Schools of Drew University, Madison, New Jersey. She is the author of *From a Broken Web: Separation, Sexism and Self*, Boston 1986, and of *Apocalypse Now and Then: A Feminist Guide to the End of the World*, Boston 1996.

Address: Drew University, The Divinity School, Madison, NJ 07940, USA.

ALEXANDER NAVA recently completed his PhD at the University of Chicago, and is currently Assistant Professor of Theology at Seattle University. His dissertation is entitled *The Mystical-Prophetic Thought of Simone Weil and Gustavo Gutierrez: Reflections on the Mystery and Hiddenness of God.*

Address: 7152 E. Brooks Dr, Tucson, AZ 85730, USA.

HANS-ECKEHARD BAHR was born in 1928. He is Emeritus Professor of Practical Theology at the Ruhr University, Bochum, and is now in charge of a project on 'Youth Violence and Peace in the City' there.

DAVID R. BLUMENTHAL is the Jay and Leslie Cohen Professor of Judaic Studies at Emory University in Atlanta, Georgia. His current interest is contemporary Jewish theology. His first work, *God at the Center*, is a book on contemporary Jewish spiritual theology rooted in the writings of the hasidic rabbi, Levi Yitzhak of Berditchev. He has also written *The Place of Faith and Grace in Judaism*; 'Mercy', 'Creation: What Difference Does It Make', and several entries in various books of Jewish, Christian, and Muslim dialogue. His second major work in contemporary Jewish theology is entitled *Facing the Abusing God: A Theology of Protest.* It draws on psychotherapy with survivors of child abuse and the Holocaust to suggest an answer to the question, where God was during the Holocaust. He is now completing his third book in this area entitled *The Banality of Good and Evil: A Social-Psychological and Theological Reflection.* It draws on social-psychological and historical research to propose an answer to the question where humanity was during the Holocaust. Much of his work is available on his website (http://www.emory.edu/UDR/BLUMENTHAL).

Address: 1669 Mason Mill Rd, Atlanta, GA 30329, USA.

DAVID TRACY was born in 1939 in Yonkers, New York. He is a priest of the diocese of Bridgeport, Connecticut, and a doctor of theology of the Gregorian University, Rome. He is The Greeley Distinguished Service Professor of Philosophical Theology at the Divinity School of Chicago University. He is the author of *The Achievement of Bernard Lonergan* (1970), *Blessed Rage for Order: New Pluralism in Theology* (1975), *The Analogical Imagination* (1980), and *Plurality and Ambiguity* (1987).

Address: University of Chicago, Divinity School Swift Hall, 1025 East 58th Street, Chicago, Ill. 60637, USA.

The editors wish to thank the great number of colleagues who contributed in a most helpful way to the final project.

J. J. Almeny	Madrid	Spain
N. A. Ančić	Split	Croatia
G. Baum	Montreal	Canada
W. Beuken	Leuven	Belgium
F. Castillo	Santiago	Chile
R. G. Cote	Ottawa	Canada
K. Derksen	Utrecht	The Netherlands
C. Duquoc	Lyons	France
M. E. Hunt	Silver Spring	USA
O. John	Ibbenbüren	Germany
R. A. Johnson	Washington, DC	USA
M. J. Mananzan	Manila	The Philippines
J. B. Metz	Vienna	Austria
M. Pilar Aquino	San Diego	USA
H. R. Schlette	Bonn	Germany
D. Singles	Lyons	France
J. M. Soskice	Cambridge	United Kingdom
P. Suess	Sao Paulo	Brazil
E. Tamez	San José	Costa Rica
J. E. Thiel	Fairfield	USA
F. Elizondo	Madrid	Spain
R. Gibellini	Brescia	France
M. Vidal	Madrid	Spain
C. Theobald	Paris	France
R. Panikkar	Barcelona	Spain
L. Sowle Cahill	Chestnut Hill	USA

JOHN TEMPLETON FOUNDATION
announces the
1998
CALL FOR EXEMPLARY PAPERS
in
HUMILITY THEOLOGY

To encourage scholarly research on matters of both spiritual and scientific significance, the John Templeton Foundation invites scholars to submit published papers on topics regarding the constructive interaction of:

- Theology and the natural sciences
- Religion and the medical sciences, or
- Religion and the behavioral sciences.

These papers must proceed from professional scholarship and display a spirit of intellectual humility, a respect for varied theological traditions, and an attitude of open-minded inquiry into the varied ways in which theology/religion and the empirical sciences can be mutually informative. Papers must have been published or accepted for publication in a peer-reviewed journal or similarly selective scholarly publication, and be accompanied by a 600-word précis (in English, even if the paper is not).

Prizes ranging from $500 to $3000 will be awarded in November 1998.
The deadline for the 1998 program is June 1, 1998.
The deadline for the 1999 program is June 1, 1999.

For full details and application form, please visit our web site, or write to:
Exemplary Papers Program Director ▪ JOHN TEMPLETON FOUNDATION
P.O. Box 8322 ▪ Radnor, Pennsylvania 19087-8322 USA
www.templeton.org

Reference: CON

CONCILIUM

The Theological Journal of the 1990s

Now available from Orbis Books

Founded in 1965 and published five times a year, *Concilium* is a world-wide journal of theology. Its editors and essayists encompass a veritable 'who's who' of theological scholars. Not only the greatest names in Catholic theology, but also exciting new voices from every part of the world, have written for this unique journal.

Concilium exists to promote theological discussion in the spirit of Vatican II, out of which it was born. It is a catholic journal in the widest sense: rooted firmly in the Catholic heritage, open to other Christian traditions and the world's faiths. Each issue of *Concilium* focusses on a theme of crucial importance and the widest possible concern for our time. With contributions from Asia, Africa, North and South America and Europe, *Concilium* truly reflects the multiple facets of the world church.

Now available from Orbis Books, *Concilium* will continue to focus theological debate and to challenge scholars and students alike.

Concilium Subscription Information - outside North America

Individual Annual Subscription (five issues): £25.00

Institution Annual Subscription (five issues): £35.00

Airmail subscriptions: add £10.00

Individual issues: £8.95 each

New subscribers please return this form:
for a two-year subscription, double the appropriate rate

(for individuals)	£25.00	(1/2 years)	. . . .
(for institutions)	£35.00	(1/2 years)	. . . .
Airmail postage outside Europe +£10.00		(1/2 years)	. . . .

Total . . . .

I wish to subscribe for one/two years as an individual/institution
(delete as appropriate)

Name/Institution . . . .

Address . . . .

. . . .

. . . .

I enclose a cheque for . . . . payable to SCM Press Ltd

Please charge my Access/Visa/Mastercard no. . . . .

Signature . . . . .Expiry Date . . . .

Please return this form to:
SCM PRESS LTD   9 - 17 St Albans Place   London   N1 0NX